JOHN OF THE CROSS

Selections from *The Dark Night* and Other Writings

Foreword by Ron Hansen

Edited and with an Introduction by Emilie Griffin

Translation by Kieran Kavanaugh, O.C.D.

HarperSanFrancisco

A Division of HarperCollinsPublishers

Book Design by Susan Rimerman

FIRST EDITION

Library of Congress Cataloging-in-Publication Data is available upon request.

ISBN 0–06–0576480
04 05 06 07 08 RRD(H) 10 9 8 7 6 5 4 3 2 1

CONTENTS

FOREWORD

I have never met anyone who felt that they prayed enough nor that they did it particularly well. Most of us who pray are admittedly humdrum at it—irregular, impatient, distracted, disconnected, vaguely dissatisfied, and frequently quitters. We are like Claudius, Hamlet's King of Denmark, who, stewing over his many sins and treacheries, finally rises from his kneeler saying, "My words fly up, my thoughts remain below. Words without thoughts never to heaven go."

Encountering John of the Cross's poetic record of his prayer is a sometimes humiliating confirmation of how far we are from intimacy with God; it's the equivalent of watching a major league pitcher in the ninth inning of a no-hitter, or of standing underneath Michelangelo as he paints the Sistine Chapel's majestic ceiling. There's the highest measure of tension and envy and awe as we see his genius on magnificent display.

His prayer is so clearly not like our own. I have had quite smidgenly mystical experiences, fleeting moments when I truly felt God was talking to, instructing, or consoling me, but they were nothing like the overpowering communions that John of the Cross writes about in these pages.

In the Jerusalem Bible's translation of Jeremiah (20:7), the prophet cries out, "You have seduced me, Yahweh, and I have let myself be seduced." God's love, which so perseveringly seeks out all of us, found in John of the Cross an acquiescent prey. We see the impact of what that meant for him in his poetry, which must

have seemed to the Carmelite friar only a feeble attempt at reca-
pitulating a profound, transforming, thrilling, even hair-raising
contact with the Holy Being.

Thomas Merton once complained in a journal that whenever
he tried to note down the greatest gifts of his prayer, he lost all
fluency and his writing was just so much paltry scribbling compared to the real thing. Our sensual experiences have such a limited vocabulary that it's small wonder that John of the Cross's
metaphors often tend toward the breathless extravagance of
courtly romance and frequently paraphrase the Egyptian love
poetry of "The Song of Songs."

With great forbearance and graciousness, John of the Cross
also explained his poetry for those who may have been seeking
an abracadabra, a Rosetta stone, any way in to replicate his tanta-
lizing tastes of the afterlife. I myself find his hints and prompts
and theorization helpful for my own seeking, but to a far greater
extent I feel affirmed and invigorated by his happiness and confi-
dence in the worth of his quest. He is like those intrepid explor-
ers who return to us starved, ruined, impoverished, frostbitten,
perhaps minus some fingers and toes, and yet are crazed with
excitement over what they'd found on the other side—the glorious, undiscovered country.

Contact with the Christ who finds us in our need, John of the
Cross tells us, cancels out anything that rejection, injury, or inhu-
manity can ever do to us. And contact with John of the Cross was
a wonderful revelation for others who served the Lord, for as the
great Carmelite reformer Teresa of Avila wrote of him, "He is a

man whose home is in heaven, full of God. I can assure you that since he went down there, I have found no one like him in all Castile. . . The sisters should open their souls to him—they will see how much good it does them."

His books were published for the first time in 1619 and are patchy and maddening in their disorder, the left-behinds of a man who did not take his writing seriously. We have only twenty-six poems, some instructions and precautions on the mystical life, a hundred or more maxims culled from his writings, the unfinished manuscripts of The Ascent of Mount Carmel and The Dark Night of the Soul, his long commentaries on the poems The Spiritual Canticle and The Living Flame of Love, and just twenty letters— a great many others having been destroyed by himself or his persecutors.

But it is enough. "Lost to all things and won over to love," John of the Cross here has given us a handbook on the freedom, simplicity, and receptivity that is the soul's ideal habitat and the door through which God enters our lives.

—RON HANSEN

INTRODUCTION

John of the Cross was a mystic, a scholar, a spiritual director, a religious superior, and above all a poet. In his poetry he captured the drama and adventure of the spiritual life. But those around him clamored for explanations, commentaries on the poems that would provide enlightenment. So John's works of instruction—*The Ascent of Mount Carmel*, *The Dark Night*, *The Spiritual Canticle*, and *The Living Flame of Love*—all are commentaries on his poems.

John was born in 1542 in the small town of Fontiveros in Spain. His father, Gonzalo de Yepes, was the son of an upper-class family of silk merchants. But they disowned Gonzalo when he married Catalina Alvarez, a poor woman of the weaving trade. Gonzalo and Catalina had three sons—John was the youngest. But Gonzalo died when John was just three. Soon John's brother Luis died as well, and Catalina was in desperate circumstances. To provide for her two sons she moved to Medina del Campo, one of Spain's great market centers. There John, aged nine, entered a school for poor children, where he soon began to excel in nursing and hospital work.

John had a chance to take Latin and rhetoric at the nearby Jesuit school and showed a flair for learning. He began to study the classics at night after his hospital work was done. The Jesuits encouraged his love of literature, and he began to write poetry.

John had a heart for the contemplative life. He entered the Carmelite monastery when he was twenty-one and plunged into Carmelite spirituality. The Carmelites encouraged his intellect by sending him to the University of Salamanca for philosophy and theology, where he excelled. Ordained a priest, he still wanted a deeper experience of contemplation and was thinking of transferring to the Carthusians for a stricter observance of silence and solitude.

But when he returned to Medina to sing his first Mass, John met a remarkable woman, a leader in the Carmelite reform. She was Teresa of Avila, who was bringing about a small revolution in Carmelite practice and spirituality. Despite the gap in their ages—Teresa was fifty-two and John twenty-five—they struck up an immediate friendship. Teresa wanted young friars to help her adapt new ways of spirituality for Carmelite men. Little Friar John (four feet, eleven inches) was just the man she needed. Teresa knew a spiritual giant when she saw one.

Teresa's movement was spreading through Spain. She was founding contemplative communities in many locations, dedicated to a strict life of poverty, enclosure, fasting, silence, and, of course, prayer. The groups were called by various names but eventually the name "discalced"—meaning "barefoot"—took hold. Teresa's Carmelites did go barefoot as a sign of radical commitment to Christ.

The Discalced Carmelites also emphasized a way of prayer called "recollection." Recollection begins with turning from the exterior life of mindless chatter and feverish activity, away from noisy and distracting people and places, toward the calm and peace of the inner life. Entering within oneself, withdrawing "into the heart," one begins, by grace, to unite the soul with the "soul's highest part," where the image of God is imprinted. In short, this kind of prayer helps to unite God and the soul.

Both Teresa of Avila and John of the Cross (he had chosen that name in 1568) were skilled organizers, planners, and doers. At the same time, both were practicing the spiritual life at a deep level. While sending John off to instruct Carmelite friars in the new ways, Teresa also contrived to retain him as spiritual director to herself and her sisters, for John was able to shepherd Teresa through many intense mystical experiences.

John's love for the spiritual life was not a result of shyness or an introverted personality. Many stories show him as an engaging conversationalist. Over his lifetime he was spiritual director to thousands, both in lay and religious life. He ministered to scandalous persons as well as the meek and respectable Carmelites.

But John's popularity had its drawbacks. Others were jealous and wanted him out of the community. In fact, the religious ferment of Spain was shot through with suspicion. Each new development was scrutinized, lest it have something to do with Protestant influence or other foreign religious ideas. Both Teresa and John were the targets of whispering campaigns. In 1574, after Teresa of Avila's term as superior ended, John offered to go elsewhere in order to minimize dissension. But his superior, papal nuncio Nicolás Ormaneto, insisted that he remain. John did so, but when Ormaneto died in 1577, John was arrested, blindfolded, and imprisoned in Toledo. He had been accused of violations of monastic obedience by his fellow monks.

John was confined to a room measuring six by ten feet. He was severely flogged, fed a diet of bread and water, and held in solitary, common punishments of the time. He was asked to renounce the Teresian way of life, which he refused to do. This time of imprisonment was for John a "dark night." During his detention, John continued to pray. He also composed poems, which became the foundation of his distinctive spiritual teaching. John had no pen and paper.

After nine months, John escaped and took refuge with Teresa's nuns in Toledo. From there, through their intervention, he went into the nearby hospital of Santa Cruz, where he was cared for. Later on, when some order had been restored and his work as a superior continued, John completed his literary work in more congenial surroundings: in the historic city of Granada, in a monastery overlooking the grandeur of the Sierra Nevada and adjacent to the property of the Alhambra, the palace of the Muslim kings. But the poems begun in prison became essential to John's way of teaching the spiritual life.

John himself says that his stanzas "include all the doctrine I intend to discuss in this book, The Ascent of Mount Carmel. They describe the way that leads to the summit of the mount—that high state of perfection we here call union of a soul with God." In The Ascent as well as in The Dark Night John deals with both purification and union. He explains to readers that he will rely on sacred Scripture for his interpretations, rather than trust his own experiences entirely.

The Spiritual Canticle is directly influenced by the Song of Songs. In John's poem, there is a dialogue between two lovers, the bridegroom and the soul, who personify the Lord Jesus and his beloved. John composed the first thirty-one stanzas in his Toledo prison cell, drawing on biblical imagery: mountains, valleys, rivers, flowers, caverns. Many of his powerful word pictures have become part of a kind of mystical language: "the wounded stag" (who symbolizes Jesus Christ, wounded by his love for us) and other remarkable images.

John was a gifted spiritual writer, but writing was not his major occupation. He was active as a superior and founder of monasteries. He also designed the monasteries at Granada and Segovia as well as an aqueduct to bring water to the Granada monastery from the Alhambra. He often took part in the actual building of the monasteries he helped to found. Over his lifetime, his formal writing, including correspondence, amounts to no more than a thousand pages. Yet in these relatively few pages a touching record of the mystical life is set forth. John of the Cross means to make God's love available to all who seriously pursue the life of prayer.

Even though he spent a lifetime as a superior, prior, founder, and director of monasteries, nevertheless his principal activity was prayer, in which remarkable graces and insights came to him. One of his most striking notions was *nada*, or "nothing," which relates to the soul's being stripped of every attachment or entanglement in order to be utterly simple and naked before God. Some may find this austere. In fact, John means to teach us simplicity of heart, which is not daunting but joyful. Those who knew him spoke of him as a man of gentle spirit, concerned for children and the poor, taking time to teach reading when the occasion demanded it to children trapped in poverty as he had once been. Always, he appreciated the beauty of the outdoors, of human companionship, of creative life.

The death of John of the Cross came about in the fateful year 1591. Once again, the inner turmoil of the Carmelite religious community was his downfall. Two friars, apparently fueled by resentment, were seeking to have him expelled from the order. The sisters were beginning to destroy his letters and correspondence, lest anything be used against him. At this time John fell seriously ill with a persistent fever and inflammation of the leg. Seeking medical help, John traveled to the town of Ubeda. Once there, he had to ask the local pastor for help, apologizing because he knew his presence was a burden on the community. The pastor, Father Crisóstomo, had no love for John and resented his arrival. But John's disease worsened—it was diagnosed as erysipelas—and the pastor's heart began to melt. John was nearing death.

At midnight on December 14, 1591, shortly after the bell rang for Matins, John died, repeating the psalm, "Into your hands, O Lord, I commend my spirit."

John of the Cross was beatified in 1675 by the Catholic church, canonized in 1726, and declared a Doctor of the Church in 1926. Because of his particular ways of dealing with suffering and lifting burdens of anxiety for others, he has received the title "Patron of the Afflicted."

—EMILIE GRIFFIN

THE DARK NIGHT

Chapter Four

The first stanza and its commentary.

One dark night,
Fired with love's urgent longings
—Ah, the sheer grace!—
I went out unseen,
My house being now all stilled.

Understanding this stanza now to refer to contemplative purgation or nakedness and poverty of spirit (which are all about the same), we can thus explain it, as though the soul says:

"Poor, abandoned, and unsupported by any of the apprehensions of my soul (in the darkness of my intellect, the distress of my will, and in the affliction and anguish of my memory), left to darkness in pure faith, which is a dark night for these natural faculties, and with only my will touched by the sorrows, afflictions, and longings of love of God, I went out from myself. That is, I departed from my low manner of understanding, and my feeble way of loving, and my poor and limited method of finding satisfaction in God. I did this unhindered by either the flesh or the devil.

"This was great happiness and a sheer grace for me, because through the annihilation and calming of my faculties, passions, appetites, and affections, by which my experience and satisfaction in God were base, I went out from my human operation and way of acting to God's operation and way of acting. That is, my intellect departed from itself, changing from human and natural to divine. For, united with God through this purgation, it no longer understands by means of its natural vigor and light, but by means of the divine wisdom to which it was united.

"And my will departed from itself and became divine. United with the divine love, it no longer loves in a lowly manner, with its natural strength, but with the strength and purity of the Holy Spirit; and thus the will does not operate humanly in relation to God."

And finally, all the strength and affections of the soul, by means of this night and purgation of the old man, are renewed with divine qualities and delights.

Chapter Five

Begins to explain how this dark contemplation is not only night for the soul, but also affliction and torment.

This dark night is an inflow of God into the soul that purges it of its habitual ignorances and imperfections, natural and spiritual, and which contemplatives call infused contemplation or mystical theology. Through this contemplation, God teaches the soul secretly and instructs it in the perfection of love without its doing anything or understanding how this happens.

Insofar as infused contemplation is loving wisdom of God, it produces two principal effects in the soul: it prepares the soul for the union with God through love by both purging and illumining it. Hence the same loving wisdom that purges and illumines the blessed spirits purges and illumines the soul here on earth.

Yet a doubt arises: Why, if it is a divine light (for it illumines souls and purges them of their ignorances), does one call it a dark night? In answer to this, there are two reasons why this divine wisdom is not only night and darkness for the soul, but also affliction and torment. First, because of the height of the divine wisdom, which exceeds the capacity of the soul. Second, because of the soul's baseness and impurity; and on this account the wisdom is painful, afflictive, and also dark for the soul.

To prove the first reason, we must presuppose a certain principle of the Philosopher: that the clearer and more obvious divine things are in themselves, the darker and more hidden they are to the soul naturally. The brighter the light, the more the owl is blinded; and the more one looks at the brilliant sun, the more the sun darkens the faculty of sight, deprives it and overwhelms it in its weakness.

Hence when the divine light of contemplation strikes souls not yet entirely illumined, it causes spiritual darkness, for it not only surpasses them, but also deprives and darkens their act of understanding. This is why St. Dionysius and other mystical theologians call this infused contemplation a ray of darkness, that is, for the soul not yet illumined and purged. For this great supernatural light overwhelms the intellect and deprives it of its natural vigor.

David also said that clouds and darkness are near God and surround him [Ps. 18:11], not because this is true in itself, but because it appears thus to our weak intellects, which in being unable to attain so bright a light are blinded and darkened. Hence, he immediately added: "Clouds passed before the great splendor of his presence" [Ps. 18:11], that is, between God and our intellect. As a result, when God communicates this bright ray of his secret wisdom to the soul not yet transformed, he causes thick darkness in its intellect.

It is also evident that this dark contemplation is painful to the soul in these beginnings. Since this divine infused contemplation has many extremely good properties, and the still unpurged soul that receives it has many extreme miseries, and because two contraries cannot coexist in one subject, the soul must necessarily undergo affliction and suffering. Because of the purgation of its imperfections caused by this contemplation, the soul becomes a battlefield in which these two contraries combat one another. We will prove this by induction in the following way.

In regard to the first cause of one's affliction: because the light and wisdom of this contemplation is very bright and pure, and the soul in which it shines is dark and impure, a person will be deeply afflicted on receiving it. When eyes are sickly, impure, and weak, they suffer pain if a bright light shines on them.

The soul, because of its impurity, suffers immensely at the time this divine light truly assails it. When this pure light strikes in order to expel all impurity, persons feel so unclean and wretched that it seems God is against them and they are against God.

Because it seems that God has rejected them, these souls suffer such pain and grief that when God tried Job in this way it proved one of the worst of Job's trials, as he says: "Why have you

set me against you, and I am heavy and burdensome to myself?"
[Job 7:20]. Clearly beholding its impurity by means of this pure
light, although in darkness, the soul understands distinctly that it
is worthy neither of God nor of any creature. And what most
grieves it is that it thinks it will never be worthy, and that there
are no more blessings for it. This divine and dark light causes
deep immersion of the mind in the knowledge and feeling of
one's own miseries and evils; it brings all these miseries into
relief, so that the soul sees clearly that of itself it will never possess anything else. We can interpret that passage from David in
this sense: "You have corrected people for their iniquity and have
undone and consumed their souls, as a spider is eviscerated in its
work" [Ps. 39:11].

Souls suffer affliction in the second manner because of their
natural, moral, and spiritual weakness. Since this divine contemplation assails them somewhat forcibly in order to subdue and
strengthen their soul, they suffer so much in their weakness that
they almost die, particularly at times when the light is more powerful. Both the sense and the spirit, as though under an immense
and dark load, undergo such agony and pain that the soul would
consider death a relief. The prophet Job, having experienced this,
declared: "I do not want him to commune with me with much
strength that he might not overwhelm me with the weight of his
greatness" [Job 23:6].

Under the stress of this oppression and weight, individuals feel
so far from all favor that they think, and so it is, that even that
which previously upheld them has ended along with everything

else, and that there is no one who will take pity on them. It is in this sense that Job also cried out: "Have pity on me, at least you my friends, for the hand of the Lord has touched me" [Job 19:21].

How amazing and pitiful it is that the soul be so utterly weak and impure that the hand of God, though light and gentle, should feel so heavy and contrary. For the hand of God does not press down or weigh on the soul, but only touches it; and this mercifully, for God's aim is to grant it favors and not chastise it.

Chapter Eight

Other afflictions that trouble the soul.

This, precisely, then, is what the divine ray of contemplation does. In striking the soul with its divine light, it surpasses the natural light and thereby darkens and deprives individuals of all the natural affections and apprehensions they perceive by means of their natural light. It leaves their spiritual and natural faculties not only in darkness, but in emptiness too. Leaving the soul thus empty and dark, the ray purges and illumines it with divine spiritual light, while the soul thinks it has no light and that it is in darkness, as illustrated in the case of the ray of sunlight that is invisible even in the middle of a room if the room is pure and void of any object on which the light may reflect. Yet when this spiritual light finds an object on which to shine, that is, when something is to be understood spiritually concerning perfection or imperfection, no matter how slight, or about a judgment on the truth or falsity of some matter, individuals will understand more clearly than they did before they were in this darkness. And easily recognizing the imperfection that presents itself, they grow conscious of the spiritual light they possess; for the ray of light is dark and invisible until a hand or some other thing passes through it, and then both the object and the ray are recognized. . . .

Chapter Nine

Although this night darkens the spirit, it does so to give light.

It remains to be said, then, that even though this happy night darkens the spirit, it does so only to impart light concerning all things. And even though it humbles persons and reveals their miseries, it does so only to exalt them. And even though it impoverishes and empties them of all possessions and natural affection, it does so only that they may reach out divinely to the enjoyment of all earthly and heavenly things, with a general freedom of spirit in them all.

That elements be commingled with all natural compounds, they must be unaffected by any particular color, odor, or taste, and thus they can concur with all tastes, odors, and colors. Similarly, the spirit must be simple, pure, and naked as to all natural affections, actual and habitual, in order to be able to freely communicate in fullness of spirit with the divine wisdom, in which, on account of the soul's purity, the delights of all things are tasted in a certain eminent degree. Without this purgation the soul would be wholly unable to experience the satisfaction of all this abundance of spiritual delight. Only one attachment or one particular object to which the spirit is actually or habitually bound is enough to hinder the experience or reception of the delicate and intimate delight of the spirit of love, which contains eminently in itself all delights. . . .

Individuals suffer these afflictive purgations of spirit that they may be reborn in the life of the spirit by means of this divine inflow, and through these sufferings the spirit of salvation is brought forth in fulfillment of the words of Isaiah: "In your presence, O Lord, we have conceived and been in the pains of labor and have brought forth the spirit of salvation" [Isa. 26:17–18].

Moreover, the soul should leave aside all its former peace because it is prepared by means of this contemplative night to attain inner peace, which is of such a quality and so delightful that, as the church says, it surpasses all understanding. That former peace was not truly peace because it was clothed with many imperfections, although to the soul walking in delight it seemed to be peace. It seemed to be a twofold peace, sensory and spiritual, since the soul beheld within itself a spiritual abundance. This sensory and spiritual peace, since it is still imperfect, must first be purged; the soul's peace must be disturbed and taken away. In the passage we quoted to demonstrate the distress of this night, Jeremiah felt disturbed and wept over his loss of peace: "My soul is withdrawn and removed from peace" [Lam. 3:17].

Chapter Ten

Explains this purgation thoroughly by means of a comparison.

For the sake of further clarity in this matter, we ought to note that this purgative and loving knowledge, or divine light we are speaking of, has the same effect on a soul that fire has on a log of wood. The soul is purged and prepared for union with the divine light just as the wood is prepared for transformation into the fire. Fire, when applied to wood, first dehumidifies it, dispelling all moisture and making it give off any water it contains. Then it gradually turns the wood black, makes it dark and ugly, and even causes it to emit a bad odor. By drying out the wood, the fire brings to light and expels all those ugly and dark accidents that are contrary to fire. Finally, by heating and enkindling it from without, the fire transforms the wood into itself and makes it as beautiful as the fire itself. Once transformed, the wood no longer has any activity or passivity of its own, except for its weight and its quantity, which is denser than the fire. For it possesses the properties and performs the actions of fire: it is dry and it dries; it is hot and it gives off heat; it is brilliant and it illumines; and it is also much lighter than before. It is the fire that produces all these properties in the wood.

Similarly, we should philosophize about this divine, loving fire of contemplation. Before transforming the soul, it purges it of all contrary qualities. It produces blackness and darkness and brings to the fore the soul's ugliness; thus the soul seems worse than before and unsightly and abominable. This divine purge stirs up all the foul and vicious humors of which the soul was never before aware. Never did it realize there was so much evil in itself, for these humors were so deeply rooted. And now that they may be expelled and annihilated they are brought to light and seen clearly through the illumination of this dark light of divine contemplation. Although the soul is no worse than before, neither in itself nor in its relationship with God, it feels undoubtedly so bad as to be not only unworthy that God should see it, but deserving of his abhorrence; in fact, it feels that God now does abhor it.

This comparison illustrates many of the things we have been saying.

First, we can understand that the very loving light and wisdom into which the soul will be transformed is that which in the beginning purges and prepares it, just as the fire which transforms the wood by incorporating it into itself is that which was first preparing it for this transformation.

Second, we discern that the experience of these sufferings does not derive from this wisdom—for as the Wise Man says: "All good things come to the soul together with her" [Wis. 7:11]—but from the soul's own weakness and imperfection. Without this purgation it cannot receive the divine light, sweetness, and delight of wisdom, just as the log of wood until prepared cannot be transformed by the fire that is applied to it. And this is why the soul suffers so intensely. Sirach confirms our assertion by telling what he suffered in order to be united with wisdom and enjoy it: "My soul wrestled for her, and my entrails were disturbed in acquiring her; therefore shall I possess a good possession" [Sir. 51:19–21].

Third, we can infer the manner in which souls suffer in purgatory. The fire, when applied, would be powerless over them if they did not have imperfections from which to suffer. These imperfections are the fuel that catches fire, and once they are gone there is nothing left to burn. So it is here on earth; when the imperfections are gone, the soul's suffering terminates, and joy remains.

Fourth, we deduce that as the soul is purged and purified by this fire of love, it is further enkindled in love, just as the wood becomes hotter as the fire prepares it. Individuals, however, do not always feel this enkindling of love. But sometimes the contemplation shines less forcibly, so that they may have the opportunity of observing and rejoicing in the work being achieved, for then these good effects are revealed. It is as though one were to stop work and take the iron out of the forge to observe what is being accomplished. Thus the soul is able to perceive the good of which it was unaware while the work was proceeding. So, too, when the flame stops acting on the wood, there is a chance to see how much the wood has been enkindled by it.

Fifth, we can also gather from this comparison why, as we previously mentioned, the soul after this alleviation suffers again, more intensely and inwardly than before. After that manifestation and after a more exterior purification of imperfections, the fire of love returns to act more interiorly on the consumable matter of which the soul must be purified. The suffering of the soul becomes more intimate, subtle, and spiritual in proportion to the inwardness, subtlety, spiritual character, and deep-rootedness of the imperfections that are removed. This more interior purgation resembles the action of fire on wood: as the fire penetrates, its action becomes stronger and more vehement, preparing the innermost part in order to gain possession of it.

Sixth, we discover the reason the soul thinks that all blessings are past and that it is full of evil, for at this time it is conscious of nothing but its own bitterness; just as in the example of the wood, for neither the air nor anything else reaches it; only the consuming fire. Yet, when other manifestations like the previous are made, the soul's joy will be more interior because of the more intimate purification.

Seventh, we deduce that when the purification is soon to return, even though the soul's joy is ample during these intervals (so much so that it sometimes seems, as we pointed out, that the bitterness will never recur), there is a feeling, if the soul adverts (and sometimes it cannot help adverting), that some root remains. And this advertence does not allow complete joy, for it seems that the purification is threatening to assail it again. And when the soul does have this feeling, the purification soon returns. Finally, that more inward part still to be purged and illumined cannot be completely concealed by the portion already purified, just as there is a very perceptible difference between that in most part of the wood still to be illumined and that which is already purged. When this purification returns to attack more interiorly, it is no wonder that once again the soul thinks all its good has come to an end and that its blessings are over. Placed in these more interior sufferings, it is blinded as to all exterior good.

With this example in mind as well as the explanation of verse 1 of the first stanza concerning this dark night and its terrible traits, it will be a good thing to leave these sad experiences and begin now to discuss the fruit of the soul's tears and the happy traits about which it begins to sing in the second verse: *Fired with love's urgent longings.*

Chapter Eleven

The beginning of an explanation of verse 2 of the first stanza. Tells how the fruit of these dark straits is a vehement passion of divine love.

In this second verse the soul refers to the fire of love that, like material fire acting on wood, penetrates it in this night of painful contemplation. Although this enkindling of love we are now discussing is in some way similar to that which occurs in the sensory part of the soul, it is as different from it in another way as is the soul from the body, or the spiritual part from the sensory part. For the enkindling of love occurs in the spirit, and through it the soul in the midst of these dark conflicts feels vividly and keenly that it is being wounded by a strong divine love, and it has a certain feeling and foretaste of God. Yet it understands nothing in particular, for as we said the intellect is in darkness.

The spirit herein experiences an impassioned and intense love because this spiritual inflaming engenders the passion of love. Since this love is infused, it is more passive than active and thus generates in the soul a strong passion of love. This love is now beginning to possess something of union with God and thereby shares to a certain extent in its properties. These properties are actions of God more than of the soul, and they reside in it passively, although the soul does give its consent. But only the love of God, which is being united to the soul, imparts the heat, strength, temper, and passion of love, or fire, as the soul terms it here. The more the soul is equipped to receive the wound and union, the more this love finds that all the soul's appetites are brought into subjection, alienated, incapacitated, and unable to be satisfied by any heavenly or earthly thing.

This happens very particularly in this dark purgation, as we said, since God so weans and recollects the appetites that they cannot find satisfaction in any of their objects. God proceeds thus so that by withdrawing the appetites from other objects and recollecting them in himself, he may strengthen the soul and give it the capacity for this strong union of love, which he begins to accord by means of this purgation. In this union the soul will love God intensely with all its strength and all its sensory and spiritual appetites. Such love is impossible if these appetites are scattered by their satisfaction in other things. In order to receive the strength of this union of love, David proclaimed to God: "I will keep my strength for you" [Ps. 59:9], that is, all the ability, appetites, and strength of my faculties, by not desiring to make use of them or find satisfaction in anything outside of you. . . .

THE SPIRITUAL CANTICLE

This commentary on the stanzas that deal
with the exchange of love between the soul
and Christ, its bridegroom, explains certain
matters about prayer and its effects. It was
written at the request of Madre Ana de Jesús,
prioress of the Discalced Carmelite nuns of
St. Joseph's in Granada, 1584.

Prologue

These stanzas, Reverend Mother, were obviously composed with a certain burning love of God. The wisdom and charity of God is so vast, as the book of Wisdom states, that it reaches from end to end [Wis. 8:1], and those informed and moved by it bear in some way this very abundance and impulsiveness in their words. As a result I do not plan to expound these stanzas in all the breadth and fullness that the fruitful spirit of love conveys to them. It would be foolish to think that expressions of love arising from mystical understanding, like these stanzas, are fully explainable. The Spirit of the Lord, who abides in us and aids our weakness, as St. Paul says [Rom. 8:26], pleads for us with unspeakable groanings in order to manifest what we can neither fully understand nor comprehend.

Who can describe the understanding he gives to loving souls in whom he dwells? And who can express the experience he imparts to them? Who, finally, can explain the desires he gives them? Certainly, no one can! Not even they who receive these communications. As a result these persons let something of their experiences overflow in figures and similes, and from the abundance of their spirit pour out secrets and mysteries rather than rational explanations.

If these similitudes are not read with the simplicity of the spirit of knowledge and love they contain, they will seem to be absurdities rather than reasonable utterances, as will those comparisons of the divine Canticle of Solomon [Song of Solomon, Song of Songs] and other books of sacred Scripture where the Holy Spirit, unable to express the fullness of his meaning in ordinary words, utters mysteries in strange figures and likenesses. The saintly doctors, no matter how much they have said or will say, can never furnish an exhaustive explanation of these figures and comparisons, since the abundant meanings of the Holy Spirit cannot be caught in words. Thus the explanation of these expressions usually contains less than what they themselves embody.

Since these stanzas, then, were composed in a love flowing from abundant mystical understanding, I cannot explain them adequately, nor is it my intention to do so. I only wish to shed some general light on them, since Your Reverence has desired this of me. I believe such an explanation will be more suitable. It is better to explain the utterances of love in their broadest sense so that individuals may derive profit from them according to the mode and capacity of their own spirit, rather than narrow them down to a meaning unadaptable to every palate. As a result, though we give some explanation of these stanzas, there is no reason to be bound to this explanation. For mystical wisdom, which comes through love and is the subject of these stanzas, need not be understood distinctly in order to cause love and affection in the soul, for it is given according to the mode of faith, through which we love God without understanding him.

I will then be very brief, although I do intend to give a lengthier explanation when necessary and where the occasion arises for a discussion of some matters concerning prayer and its effects. Since these stanzas refer to many of the effects of prayer, I ought to treat at least some of these effects.

Yet, passing over the more common effects, I will deal briefly with the more extraordinary ones, which take place in those who with God's help have passed beyond the state of beginners. I do this for two reasons: first, because there are many writings for beginners; second, because I am addressing Your Reverence, at your request. And our Lord has favored you and led you beyond the state of beginners into the depths of his divine love.

I hope that, although some scholastic theology is used here in reference to the soul's interior converse with God, it will not prove vain to speak in such a manner to the pure of spirit. Even though Your Reverence lacks training in scholastic theology, by which the divine truths are understood, you are not wanting in mystical theology, which is known through love and by which one not only knows, but at the same time experiences.

And that my explanations—which I desire to submit to anyone with better judgment than mine and entirely to Holy Mother the Church—may be worthy of belief, I do not intend to affirm anything of myself or trust in any of my own experiences or in those of other spiritual persons whom I have known or heard of. Although I plan to make use of these experiences, I want to explain and confirm at least the more difficult matters through passages from sacred Scripture. In using these passages, I will quote the words in Latin, and then interpret them in regard to the matter being discussed.

I will now record the stanzas in full and then in due order quote each one separately before its explanation; similarly, I will quote each verse before commenting on it.

Stanzas Between the Soul and the Bridegroom

Bride

1. Where have you hidden,
Beloved, and left me moaning?
You fled like the stag
After wounding me;
I went out calling you, and you were gone.

2. Shepherds, you that go
Up through the sheepfolds to the hill,
If by chance you see
Him I love most,
Tell him that I sicken, suffer, and die.

3. Seeking my love
I will head for the mountains and for water-
sides,
I will not gather flowers,
Nor fear wild beasts;
I will go beyond strong men and frontiers.

4. O woods and thickets
Planted by the hand of my beloved!
O green meadow,
Coated, bright with flowers.
Tell me, has he passed by you?

5. Pouring out a thousand graces,
He passed these groves in haste;
And having looked at them,

With his image alone,
Clothed them in beauty.

6. Ah, who has the power to heal me?
Now wholly surrender yourself!
Do not send me
Any more messengers,
They cannot tell me what I must hear.

7. All who are free
Tell me a thousand graceful things of you;
All wound me more
And leave me dying
Of, ah, I-don't-know-what behind their stam-
mering.

8. How do you endure
O life, not living where you live?
And being brought near death
By the arrows you receive
From that which you conceive of your beloved.

9. Why, since you wounded
This heart, don't you heal it?
And why, since you stole it from me,
Do you leave it so,
And fail to carry off what you have stolen?

10. Extinguish these miseries,
Since no one else can stamp them out;
And may my eyes behold you,

Because you are their light,
And I would open them to you alone.

11. Reveal your presence,
And may the vision of your beauty be my
death;
For the sickness of love
Is not cured
Except by your very presence and image.

12. O spring like crystal!
If only, on your silvered-over face,
You would suddenly form
The eyes I have desired,
Which I bear sketched deep within my heart.

13. Withdraw them, beloved,
I am taking flight!

Bridegroom

Return, dove,
The wounded stag
Is in sight on the hill,
Cooled by the breeze of your flight.

Bride

14. My beloved, the mountains
And lonely wooded valleys,
Strange islands,

And resounding rivers,
The whistling of love-stirring breezes,

15. The tranquil night
At the time of the rising dawn,
Silent music,
Sounding solitude,
The supper that refreshes, and deepens love.

16. Catch us the foxes,
For our vineyard is now in flower,
While we fashion a cone of roses
Intricate as the pine's;
And let no one appear on the hill.

17. Be still, deadening north wind;
South wind come, you that waken love,
Breathe through my garden,
Let its fragrance flow,
And the beloved will feed amid the flowers.

18. You girls of Judea,
While among flowers and roses
The amber spreads its perfume,
Stay away, there on the outskirts:
Do not so much as seek to touch our thresholds.

19. Hide yourself, my love;
Turn your face toward the mountains,
And do not speak;

But look at those companions
Going with her through strange
islands.

Bridegroom

20. Swift-winged birds,
Lions, stags, and leaping roes,
Mountains, lowlands, and river banks,
Waters, winds, and ardors,
Watching fears of night:

21. By the pleasant lyres
And the siren's song, I conjure you
To cease your anger
And not touch the wall,
That the bride may sleep in deeper
peace.

22. The bride has entered
The sweet garden of her desire,
And she rests in delight,
Laying her neck
On the gentle arms of her beloved.

23. Beneath the apple tree:
There I took you for my own,
There I offered you my hand,
And restored you,
Where your mother was corrupted.

Bride

24. Our bed is in flower,
Bound round with linking dens of lions,
Hung with purple,
Built up in peace,
And crowned with a thousand shields of gold.

25. Following your footprints
Maidens run along the way;
The touch of a spark,
The spiced wine,
Cause flowings in them from the sacred balsam.

26. In the inner wine cellar
I drank of my beloved, and when I went abroad
Through all this valley
I no longer knew anything,
And lost the herd that I was following.

27. There he gave me his breast;
There he taught me a sweet and living
knowledge;
And I gave myself to him,
Keeping nothing back;
There I promised to be his bride.

28. Now I occupy my soul
And all my energy in his service;
I no longer tend the herd,

Nor have I any other work
Now that my every act is love.

29. If, then, I am no longer
Seen or found on the common,
You will say that I am lost;
That, stricken by love,
I lost myself, and was found.

30. With flowers and emeralds
Chosen on cool mornings
We shall weave garlands
Flowering in your love,
And bound with one hair of mine.

31. You considered
That one hair fluttering at my neck;
You gazed at it upon my neck;
And it captivated you;
And one of my eyes wounded you.

32. When you looked at me
Your eyes imprinted your grace in me;
For this you loved me ardently;
And thus my eyes deserved
To adore what they beheld in you.

33. Do not despise me;
For if, before, you found me dark,
Now truly you can look at me

Since you have looked
And left in me grace and beauty.

Bridegroom

34. The small white dove
Has returned to the ark with an olive branch;
And now the turtledove
Has found its longed-for mate
By the green river banks.

35. She lived in solitude,
And now in solitude has built her nest;
And in solitude he guides her,
He alone, who also bears
In solitude the wound of love.

Bride

36. Let us rejoice, beloved,
And let us go forth to behold ourselves in your
beauty,
To the mountain and to the hill,
To where the pure water flows,
And further, deep into the thicket.

37. And then we will go on
To the high caverns in the rock
Which are so well concealed;
There we shall enter
And taste the fresh juice of the pomegranates.

38. There you will show me
What my soul has been seeking,
And then you will give me,
You, my life, will give me there
What you gave me on that other day:

39. The breathing of the air,
The song of the sweet nightingale,
The grove and its living beauty
In the serene night,
With a flame that is consuming and painless.

40. No one looked at her,
Nor did Aminadab appear;
The siege was still;
And the cavalry,
At the sight of the waters, descended.

Stanza 10

Introduction

The soul, then, in this condition of love is like those who are sick, who are extremely tired and, having lost their taste and appetite, find all food nauseating and everything a disturbance and annoyance. In everything they think about or see they have only one desire, the desire for health, and all that does not lead to health is a bother and a burden to them.

Since the soul has reached this sickness of love of God, she has three traits. The first is that in all things that are offered to her, or with which she deals, she has ever before her that longing for her health, which is her beloved. Even though she cannot help being occupied with them, she always has her heart fixed on him. The second trait, arising from this first, is the loss of taste for all things. The third, then, results, which is that all these things molest her and that all dealings with others are burdensome and annoying.

The reason for these traits, deduced from what has been said, is that, since the palate of the soul's will has tasted this food of love of God, her will is inclined immediately to seek and enjoy her beloved in everything that happens and in all her occupations, without looking for any satisfaction or concern of her own. Mary Magdalene acted similarly when with ardent love she was searching for him in the garden. Thinking that he was the gardener, without any further reasoning or considerations, she pleaded with him: "If you have taken him from me, tell me, and I will take him away" [John 20:15]. Having a similar yearning to find him in all things, and not immediately finding him as she desires—but rather quite the contrary—not only does the soul fail to find satisfaction in these things, but they also become a torment to her, and sometimes a very great one. Such souls suffer much in dealing with people and with business matters, for these contacts hinder rather than help them to their goal.

The bride clearly indicates in the Canticle these three traits she had when searching for her bridegroom: "I looked for him and did not find him. But they who go about the city found me and wounded me, and the guards of the walls took my mantle from me" [Song of Sol. 5:6–7]. Those who go about the city refer to the affairs of the world. When they find the soul who is searching for God, they inflict on her many wounds of sorrow, pain, and displeasure, for not only does she fail to find her desire in them, but she is also impeded by them. Those who guard the wall of contemplation, to prevent the soul from entering, are the devils and the negotiations of the world, and they take away the mantle of the peace and quietude of loving contemplation.

The soul that loves God derives a thousand displeasures and annoyances from all of these. Conscious that as long as she is in this life without the vision of God, she cannot free herself from them to either a small or a great degree, she continues her prayers to the beloved and recites the following stanza:

> Extinguish these miseries,
> Since no one else can stamp them out;
> And may my eyes behold you,
> Because you are their light,
> And I would open them to you alone.

Commentary

She continues in this stanza to ask the beloved to put an end to her longings and pains since he alone can do this, and no one else; and to accomplish this so that the eyes of her soul may be able to see him, since he alone is the light they behold, and she wants to employ them in him alone:

Extinguish these miseries. A characteristic of the desires of love is that all deeds and words unconformed with what the will loves, weary, tire, annoy, and displease the soul as she beholds that her desire goes unfulfilled. She refers to this weariness that she suffers in order to see God as "these miseries." And nothing but possession of the beloved can extinguish them. She says he extinguishes them by his presence and refreshes her as cool water soothes a person exhausted from the heat. She uses the word "extinguish" to indicate that she is suffering from the fire of love.

Since no one else can stamp them out. To further urge and persuade her beloved to grant her petition, she declares that, since he alone suffices to satisfy her need, he must be the one to extinguish these miseries. It is noteworthy that God is very ready to comfort and satisfy the soul in her needs and afflictions when she neither has nor desires consolation and satisfaction outside of him. The soul, possessing nothing that might withhold her from God, cannot remain long without a visit from the beloved.

And may my eyes behold you. That is: "May I see you face to face with the eyes of my soul."

Because you are their light. Regardless of the fact that God is the supernatural light of the soul's eyes, and that without this light she is enveloped in darkness, she affectionately calls him here the light of her eyes, just as any lover might call the one she loves the light of her eyes in order to show her affection.

These two verses are like saying: "Since my eyes have no other light (neither through nature nor through love) than you, may my eyes behold you, because you are their light in every way." David noted the absence of this light when he lamented: "The light of my eyes itself is not with me" [Ps. 38:10]. Tobit did the same: "What joy can be mine since I am seated in darkness and do not see the light of heaven?" [Tob. 5:10]. Through these words he gave expression to his desire for the clear vision of God, because the light of heaven is the Son of God, as St. John says: "The heavenly city has no need of the sun or of the moon to shine in it, because the brightness of God illumines it, and the Lamb is the lamp thereof" [Rev. 21:23].

And I would open them to you alone. With this line the soul desires to oblige the bridegroom to reveal this light of her eyes, not only because she lives in darkness in that her eyes have no other light, but also because she wants to keep her eyes for him alone. As the soul longing to focus the eyes of her will on the light of something outside of God is justly deprived of the divine light—insofar as the spiritual powers she has for receiving God's light are occupied with this other light—so also does the soul that closes its eyes to all things in order to open them to God alone merits congruously the illumination of the divine light.

Stanza 11

Introduction

It should be known that the loving bridegroom of souls cannot long watch them suffering alone—as this soul is suffering—because as he says through Zechariah, their afflictions touch him in the apple of his eye [Zech. 2:8]; especially when these afflictions are the outcome of love for him, as are those of this soul. He also declares through Isaiah: "Before they call, I will hear; while they are yet with the word in their mouth, I will hear them" [Isa. 65:24]. The Wise Man says of him, that if the soul seeks him as money, she will find him [Prov. 2:4–5].

Apparently God granted a certain spiritual feeling of his presence to this loving soul whose prayers are so enkindled and who seeks him more covetously than one would seek money, since she has left herself and all things for him. In this spiritual sense of his presence, he revealed some deep glimpses of his divinity and beauty by which he greatly increased her fervor and desire to see him. As a man throws water into the forge to stir up and intensify the fire, so the Lord usually grants to some souls that walk in these fiery longings of love certain signs of his excellence to make them more fervent and further prepare them for the favors he wishes to grant them later.

Since the soul saw and experienced through that obscure presence the supreme good and beauty hidden there, she recites the following stanza, dying with the desire to see him:

> Reveal your presence,
> And may the vision of your beauty be my death;
> For the sickness of love
> Is not cured
> Except by your very presence and image.

Commentary

The soul desiring to be possessed by this immense God, for love of whom she feels that her heart is robbed and wounded, unable to endure her sickness any longer, deliberately asks him in this stanza to show her his beauty, his divine essence, and to kill her with this revelation, and thereby free her from the flesh, since she cannot see and enjoy him as she wants. She makes this request by displaying before him the sickness and yearning of her heart, in which she [endures] suffering for love of him, unable to find a cure in anything less than this glorious vision of his divine essence. The verse follows:

Reveal your presence. In explanation of this verse it should be known that God's presence can be of three kinds:

The first is his presence by essence. In this way he is present not only in the holiest souls, but also in sinners and in all other creatures. For with this presence he gives them life and being. Should this essential presence be lacking to them, they would all be annihilated. Thus this presence is never wanting to the soul.

The second is his presence by grace, in which he abides in the soul, pleased and satisfied with it. Not all have this presence of God; those who fall into mortal sin lose it. The soul cannot know naturally if it has this presence.

The third is his presence by spiritual affection, for God usually grants his spiritual presence to devout souls in many ways, by which he refreshes, delights, and gladdens them.

Yet these many kinds of spiritual presence, just as the others, are all hidden, for in them God does not reveal himself as he is, since the conditions of this life will not allow such a manifestation. Thus the above verse, "reveal your presence," could be understood of any of these three ways in which God is present.

Since it is certain that at least in the first way God is ever present in the soul, she does not ask him to be present in her, but that he so reveal his hidden presence, whether natural, spiritual, or affective, that she may be able to see him in his divine being and beauty. As he gives the soul natural being through his essential presence, and perfects her through his presence by grace, she begs him to glorify her also with his manifest glory.

Yet insofar as this soul is full of fervor and tender love of God, we should understand that this presence she asks the beloved to reveal refers chiefly to a certain affective presence which the beloved accords her. This presence is so sublime that the soul feels an immense hidden being is there from which God communicates to her some semiclear glimpses of his divine beauty. And these bear such an effect on the soul that she ardently longs and faints with desire for what she feels hidden there in that presence, which is similar to what David felt when he exclaimed: "My soul longs and faints for the courts of the Lord" [Ps. 84:2].

At this time the soul faints with longing to be engulfed in that supreme good she feels present and hidden, for although it is hidden she has a notable experience of the good and delight present there. Accordingly, she is drawn and carried toward this good more forcibly than any material object is pulled toward its center by gravity. With this longing and heartfelt desire, unable to contain herself any longer, the soul begs: "Reveal your presence."

Moses had this very experience on Mount Sinai. While standing in God's presence, he was able to get such sublime and profound glimpses of the height and beauty of the hidden divinity that, unable to endure it, he asked God twice to reveal his glory: "You say that you know me by name and that I have found favor before you. If therefore I have found favor in your presence, show me your face that I may know you and find before your eyes the grace that I desire fulfilled" [Exod. 33:12–13]—that is, to reach the perfect love of the glory of God. Yet the Lord answered: "You shall not be able to see my face, for no one shall see me and live" [Exod. 33:20]. This is like saying: "You ask a difficult thing of me, Moses, for such is the beauty of my face and the delight derived from the sight of my being that your soul will be unable to withstand it in a life as weak as this."

The soul knows that she cannot see him in his beauty in this kind of life. She knows this either through God's answer to Moses or through her experience of what is hidden here in the presence of God. For even though he appears but vaguely, she faints. Hence she anticipates the reply that can be made to her as it was to Moses and says:

And may the vision of your beauty be my death. This is like saying: "Since the delight arising from the sight of your being and beauty is unendurable, and since I must die in seeing you, may the vision of your beauty be my death."

It is known that there are two visions that will kill a person because of the inability of human nature to suffer their force and vigor. One is that of the basilisk, from which it is said one dies immediately; the other is the vision of God. Yet the causes are very different, for the sight of one kills with a terrible poison, and that of God by an immense health and glorious good.

The soul does nothing very outstanding by wanting to die at the sight of the beauty of God in order to enjoy him forever. Were she to have but a foreglimpse of the height and beauty of God, she would not only desire death in order to see him now forever, as she here desires, but she would very gladly undergo a thousand singularly bitter deaths to see him only for a moment; and having seen him, she would ask to suffer just as many more that she might see him for another moment.

To shed further light on this verse, it should be known that when the soul asks that the vision of his beauty be her death, she speaks conditionally, under the supposition that she cannot see him without dying. Were she able to see him without dying, she would not ask him to slay her, for to desire death is a natural imperfection. Yet with the supposition that this corruptible life of humans is incompatible with the other incorruptible life of God, she says: "May the vision of your beauty be my death."

St. Paul teaches this doctrine to the Corinthians, saying: "We do not wish to be unclothed, but we desire to be clothed over, that that which is mortal may be absorbed in life" [2 Cor. 5:4]. This is like saying: "We do not desire to be despoiled of the flesh but to be clothed over with glory." Yet observing that one cannot live simultaneously in glory and in the mortal flesh, he says to the Philippians that he desires to be loosed and to be with Christ [Phil. 1:23]. . . .

Death cannot be bitter to the soul that loves, for in it she finds all the sweetness and delight of love. The thought of death cannot sadden her, for she finds that gladness accompanies this thought. Neither can the thought of death be burdensome and painful to her, for death will put an end to all her sorrows and afflictions and be the beginning of all her bliss. She thinks of death as her friend and bridegroom, and at the thought of it she rejoices as she would over the thought of her betrothal and marriage, and she longs for that day and that hour of her death more than earthly kings long for kingdoms and principalities.

The Wise Man proclaims of this kind of death: "O death! Your sentence is welcome to the one who feels need" [Sir. 41:2]. If it is welcome to those who feel need for earthly things, even though it does not provide for these needs but rather despoils these persons of the possessions they have, how much better will its sentence be for the soul in need of love, as is this one who is crying out for more love. For death will not despoil her of the love she possesses, but rather be the cause of love's completeness, which she desires, and the satisfaction of all her needs.

The soul is right in daring to say, "May the vision of your beauty be my death," since she knows that at the instant she sees this beauty she will be carried away by it, and absorbed in this very beauty, and transformed in this same beauty, and made beautiful like this beauty itself, and enriched and provided for like this very beauty.

David declares, consequently, that the death of the saints is precious in the sight of the Lord [Ps. 116:15]. This would not be true if they did not participate in his very grandeurs, for in the sight of god nothing is precious but what he in himself is. Accordingly, the soul does not fear death when she loves; rather, she desires it. Yet sinners are always fearful of death. They foresee that death will take everything away and bring them all evils. As David says, "The death of sinners is very evil" [Ps. 34:21]. And hence, as the Wise Man says, the remembrance of it is bitter [Sir. 41:1]. Since sinners love the life of this world intensely and have little love for that of the other, they have an immense fear of death.

The soul that loves God lives more in the next life than in this, for the soul lives where it loves more than where it gives life, and thus has but little esteem for this temporal life. She says then: "May the vision of your beauty be my death."

> For the sickness of love
> Is not cured
> Except by your very presence and image.

The reason lovesickness has no other remedy than the presence and the image of the beloved is that, since this sickness differs from others, its medicine also differs. In other sicknesses, following sound philosophy, contraries are cured by contraries, but love is incurable except by what is in accord with love.

The reason for this is that love of God is the soul's health, and the soul does not have full health until love is complete. Sickness is nothing but a want of health, and when the soul has not even a single degree of love, she is dead. But when she possesses some degrees of love of God no matter how few, she is then alive, yet very weak and infirm because of her little love. In the measure that love increases she will be healthier, and when love is perfect she will have full health.

It should be known that love never reaches perfection until the lovers are so alike that one is transfigured in the other. And then the love is in full health. The soul experiences within herself a certain sketch of love, which is the sickness she mentions, and she desires the completion of the sketch of this image, the image of her bridegroom, the Word, the Son of God, who, as St. Paul says, is the "splendor of his glory and the image of his substance" [Heb. 1:3], for this is the image referred to in this verse and into which the soul desires to be transfigured through love. As a result she says: "For the sickness of love is not cured except by your very presence and image."

She does well to call imperfect love "sickness." For just as a sick person is too weak for work, so is the soul, feeble in love, too weak to practice heroic virtue.

It is also noteworthy that those who feel in themselves the sickness of love, a lack of love, show that they have some love, because they are aware of what they lack through what they have. Those who do not feel this sickness show that they either have no love or are perfect in love.

Stanza 12

Introduction

At this period the soul feels that she is rushing toward God as impetuously as a falling stone when nearing its center. She also feels that she is like wax in which an impress is being made, but not yet completed. She knows too that she is like a sketch or the first draft of a drawing and calls out to the one who did this sketch to finish the painting and image. And her faith is so enlightened that it gives her a glimpse of some clear divine reflections of the height of her God. As a result she does not know what to do other than turn to this very faith, which contains and hides the image and the beauty of her beloved, and from which she also receives these sketches and tokens of love, and speak to it in the following stanza:

O spring like crystal!
If only, on your silvered-over face,
You would suddenly form
The eyes I have desired,
Which I bear sketched deep within my
heart. . . .

Commentary

Since the soul longs so ardently for union with the bridegroom and is aware that she finds no remedy in any creature, she turns to speak to faith, as to that which most vividly sheds light concerning her beloved, and takes it as a means toward this union. Indeed, there is no other means by which one reaches true union and spiritual espousal with God, as Hosea indicates: "I will espouse you to me in faith" [Hos. 2:20]. With this burning desire she exclaims the following, which is the meaning of the stanza: "O faith of Christ, my Spouse, would that you might show me clearly now the truths of my beloved, which you have infused in my soul and which are covered with obscurity and darkness (for faith, as the theologians say, is an obscure habit), in such a way that, what you communicate to me in inexplicit and obscure knowledge, you would show suddenly, clearly, and perfectly, changing it into a manifestation of glory! Would that you might do this by drawing back from these truths (for faith is the veil of the truths of God)!" The verse then runs:

O spring like crystal! She says faith is like crystal for two reasons: first, because it concerns Christ, her spouse; second, because it has the characteristics of crystal. It is pure in its truths, and strong and clear, cleansed of errors and natural forms.

And she calls it a spring because from it the waters of all spiritual goods flow into the soul. Christ, our Lord, speaking with the Samaritan woman, called faith a spring, declaring that in those who believed in him he would make a fountain whose waters would leap up unto life everlasting [John 4:14]. This water was the Spirit, which believers were to receive through faith [John 7:39].

If only, on your silvered-over face. She calls the propositions and articles of faith a silvered-over face. To understand this verse as well as the others, it should be known that faith is compared to silver in the propositions it teaches us, and that the truths and substance it contains are compared to gold. For in the next life we shall see and enjoy openly this very substance that, clothed and covered with the silver of faith, we now believe. . . .

Faith, consequently, gives us God, but covered with the silver of faith. Yet it does not for this reason fail to give him to us truly. Were we to be given a gold vase plated with silver, we would not fail to receive a gold vase merely because of the silver plating. God promised the bride of the Song of Songs who wanted this possession of him that, insofar as possible in this life, he would make her gold earrings plated with silver [Song of Sol. 1:10]. He thereby promised to give himself to her, but hidden in faith.

The soul, then, exclaims to faith: "Oh, if only on your silvered-over face (the articles we mentioned) by which you cover the gold of the divine rays (the eyes I have desired)," and she adds:

> You would suddenly form
> The eyes I have desired

The eyes refer to the divine truths and rays. Faith, as we mentioned, proposes these truths to us in its covered and inexplicit articles. The soul, in other words, says: "Oh, if only the truths hidden in your articles, which you teach me in an inexplicit and dark manner, you would give me now completely, clearly, and explicitly, freed of their covering, as my desire begs!"

She calls these truths eyes because of the remarkable presence of the beloved she experiences. It seems that he is now always looking at her. Thus she says:

Which I bear sketched deep within my heart. She says these truths are sketched deep within her, that is, in her soul, in her intellect and will.

For these truths are infused by faith into her intellect. And since the knowledge of them is imperfect, she says they are sketched. Just as a sketch is not a perfect painting, so the knowledge of faith is not perfect knowledge. Hence, the truths infused in the soul through faith are as though sketched, and when they will be clearly visible, they will be like a perfect and finished painting in the soul. As the Apostle says: *Cum autem venerit quod perfectum est evacuabitur quod ex parte est* [1 Cor. 13:10]; this means that when what is perfect, the clear vision, comes, that which is in part, the knowledge of faith, will end. . . .

The soul's state at this time is such that, regardless of the fact that it is indescribable, I do not want to neglect saying something about it even though briefly. It seems to the soul that its bodily and spiritual substance is drying up with thirst for this living spring of God. Its thirst is like David's when he said: "As the hart longs for the fount of waters, so does my soul long for you, my God. My soul has thirsted for God, the living fount; when shall I see and appear before the face of God?" [Ps. 42:1–2]. This thirst so exhausts the soul that she would think nothing of breaking through the midst of the camp of the Philistines, as did David's strong men, to fill their containers with water from the cistern of Bethlehem, which was Christ [1 Chron. 11:18]. She would consider all the difficulties of this world, and the fury of demons, and infernal afflictions nothing if by passing through them she could plunge into the unfathomable spring of love. In this respect it is said in the Song of Songs: "Love is as strong as death and its jealousy as hard as hell" [Song of Sol. 8:6].

It is incredible how ardent the longing and pain is that the soul experiences when she sees that she is near the enjoyment of that good, and that yet it is not given to her. The more the object of her desire comes into sight and the closer it draws, while yet being denied her, so much more pain and torment does it cause. In this spiritual sense Job says: "Before I eat, I sigh; and the roaring and bellowing of my soul is like overflowing waters" [Job 3:24], with craving for food. By the food is meant God, and the craving for food, or for the knowledge of God, is commensurate with the suffering for him.

Stanza 13

Introduction

This is the reason the soul's suffering for God at this time is so intense: she is drawing nearer to him, and so she has greater experience within herself of the void of God, of very heavy darkness, and of spiritual fire, which dries up and purges her, so that thus purified she may be united with him. Inasmuch as God does not communicate some supernatural ray of light from himself, he is intolerable darkness to her when he is spiritually near her, for the supernatural light darkens with its excess the natural light. David indicated all this when he said: "Clouds and darkness are round about him; fire goes before him" [Ps. 97:2–3]. In another psalm he asserts: "He made darkness his covert and biding place, and his tent round about him is dark water in the clouds of the air; because of his great splendor there are in his presence clouds, hail and coals of fire" [Ps. 18:11–12], that is, for the soul drawing near him. As the soul comes closer to him, and until god introduces her into his divine splendors through transformation of love, she experiences within herself all that David described. In the meanwhile, like Job, she exclaims over and over: "Who will grant me to know him and find him and come unto his throne?" [Job 23:3].

God through his immense mercy grants the soul favors and consolations in the measure of her darknesses and voids, for *sicut tenebrae ejus ita et lumen ejus* ["As its darkness left its light"] [Ps. 139:12], and in exalting and glorifying her he humbles and wearies her. In a like way he sends the soul suffering these fatigues some of his divine rays with such strong love and glory that he stirs her completely and causes her to go out of her senses. Thus in great fear and trembling, she spoke to her beloved the first part of the following stanza, and her beloved then spoke the remaining verses:

> Withdraw them, beloved,
> I am taking flight!

Bridegroom

> Return, dove,
> The wounded stag
> Is in sight on the hill,
> Cooled by the breeze of your flight.

Commentary

The beloved usually visits his bride chastely, delicately, and with strong love amid the intense loving desires and ardors she has shown in the previous stanzas. God's favors and visits are generally in accord with the intensity of the yearnings and ardors of love that precede them.

Since, as the soul just finished saying in the previous stanza, she desired these divine eyes with such yearnings, the beloved revealed to her some rays of his grandeur and divinity. He communicated these so sublimely and forcibly that he carried her out of herself in rapture and ecstasy. At the beginning this is accompanied by great pain and fear in the sensory part. Unable in her weakness to endure such excess, she proclaims in this stanza:

"Withdraw them, beloved," that is, these your divine eyes, "for they cause me to take flight and go out of myself to supreme contemplation, which is beyond what the sensory part can endure." This flight from the body is what she desired; this is why she begged him to withdraw his eyes, to cease communicating them to her in the body, in which she is unable to suffer and enjoy them as she would, and communicate them to her in her flight outside the body.

The bridegroom then impedes this desire and flight, saying: "Return, dove, for the communication you receive from me is not yet of the state of glory to which you now aspire. Return to me, for I am he whom you, wounded with love, seek. For I too, like the stag, wounded by your love, begin to reveal myself to you in your high contemplation, and I am refreshed and renewed in the love which arises from your contemplation."

The soul, then, says to the bridegroom:

Withdraw them, beloved. As we mentioned, the soul in accordance with her intense desire for these divine eyes, for the divinity, received interiorly from the beloved such divine communication and knowledge that she had to say: "Withdraw them, beloved."

The misery of human nature is such that when the communication and knowledge of the beloved, which gives more life to the soul and for which she longs so ardently, is about to be imparted, she cannot receive it save almost at the cost of her life. When she receives the eyes she has been searching for so anxiously and in so many ways, she cries: "Withdraw them, beloved!"

The torment experienced in these rapturous visits is such that there is no other which so disjoins the bones and endangers the sensory part. Were God not to provide, she would die. And indeed, it seems so to the soul in which this happens, that she is being loosed from the flesh and is abandoning the body.

The reason for this is that such favors cannot be received wholly in the body, for the spirit is elevated to commune with the divine Spirit, who comes to the soul. Thus the soul must in some fashion abandon the body. As a result the body must suffer and, consequently, the soul in the body, because of their unity in one *suppositum* [whole human being]. The torment she experiences at the time of this visit and the terror arising from her awareness of being treated in this supernatural way make her cry: "Withdraw them, beloved!"

Yet it should not be thought that because she says "withdraw them," she desires him to do so. Those words spring from natural fear, as we said. No matter what the cost, she would not want to lose these visits and favors of the beloved. Although the sensory part suffers, the spirit takes flight to supernatural recollection and enjoyment of the beloved's Spirit, which is what she desired and sought. Yet she would not want to receive the Spirit in the body, for there she cannot receive him fully, but only in a small degree and with considerable suffering. But she would want to receive him in the flight of the spirit, outside the body, where she can freely rejoice with him. Accordingly, she says, "Withdraw them, beloved," that is, "Cease communicating them to me in the body."

I am taking flight! This is like saying: "I am taking flight from the body in order that you may communicate them to me outside of it, since they cause me to fly out of the body."

For a better understanding of the nature of this flight, it should be noted that, as we said, in this visit of the divine Spirit, the spirit of the soul is carried away violently to communicate with him, and it abandons the body and ceases to have its feelings and actions in it, for they are in God. Thus St. Paul said that in his rapture he did not know if his soul was receiving the communication in the body or out of the body [2 Cor. 12:2].

However, it should not be thought because of this that the soul forsakes the body, which is its sensory life, but rather that the soul's actions are not in the body. This is why in these raptures and flights the body has no feeling, and even though severely painful things are done to it, it does not feel them. This rapture is not like other natural transports and swoons in which one returns to self when pain is inflicted.

These feelings are experienced in such visits by those who have not yet reached the state of perfection, but are advancing along in the state of proficients. Those who have reached perfection receive all communications in peace and gentle love. These raptures then cease, for they are communications preparatory to the reception of the total communication.

This would be an apt place to treat the different kinds of raptures, ecstasies, and other elevations and flights of the soul that are customarily experienced by spiritual persons. But since, as I promised in the prologue, my intention is only to give a brief explanation of these stanzas, such a discussion will have to be left for someone who knows how to treat the matter better than I. Then too, the blessed Teresa of Jesus, our Mother, left writings about these spiritual matters, which are admirably done and which I hope will soon be printed and brought to light.

What the soul then says about flight here should be understood in reference to rapture and ecstasy of the spirit in God.

And the beloved then says:

Return, dove. The soul went out of the body very willingly in that spiritual flight and thought that now her life was at an end and that she would be able to see her bridegroom openly and enjoy him forever. But the bridegroom intercepted her flight saying, "Return, dove." This is like saying: "In your sublime and swift contemplation and in your burning love and in the simplicity of your advance—for the dove has three properties—return from this lofty flight in which you aim after true possession of me; the time has not yet come for such high knowledge, adapt yourself to this lower knowledge that I am communicating to you in this rapture of yours." And it is as follows:

The wounded stag. The bridegroom in this verse compares himself to a stag. It is characteristic of the stag to climb to high places and, when wounded, to race in search of refreshment and cool waters. If he hears the cry of his mate and senses that she is wounded, he immediately runs to her to comfort and coddle her.

The bridegroom now acts similarly. Beholding that the bride is wounded with love for him, he also, because of her moan, is wounded with love for her. Among lovers, the wound of one is a wound for both, and the two have but one feeling. Thus, in other words, he says: "Return to me, my bride, because if you go about wounded with love for me, I too, like the stag, will come to you wounded by your wound."

"Also, by appearing in a high place I am like the stag." Hence he says, the stag

Is in sight on the hill, that is, "in the height of your contemplation in this flight." For contemplation is a high place where God in this life begins to communicate and show himself to the soul, but not completely. Hence he does not say that he is fully in sight, but that he is in sight. However sublime may be the knowledge God gives the soul in this life, it is but like a glimpse of him from a great distance. The third characteristic of the stag, contained in the next verse, follows:

Cooled by the breeze of your flight. By the "flight," he means the contemplation received in that ecstasy, and by the "breeze," the spirit of love that this flight of contemplation causes in the soul. He very appropriately terms this love that is caused by the flight a breeze, because the Holy Spirit, who is Love, is also compared to a breeze in Scripture, for the Holy Spirit is the breath of the Father and the Son. And just as the Holy Spirit is like a breeze from the flight (that is, he proceeds through spiration from the contemplation and wisdom of the Father and the Son), so the bridegroom calls this love of the soul a breeze, because it proceeds from the contemplation and knowledge that she has of God at this time.

It is noteworthy that the bridegroom does not say he comes at the flight, but at the breeze of the flight, because, properly speaking, God does not communicate himself to the soul through its flight (the knowledge it has of him), but through the love it has from this knowledge. For just as love is the union of the Father and the Son, so it is the union of the soul with God. Hence it is that even though a soul may have the highest knowledge and contemplation of God and know all mysteries, yet if it does not love, this knowledge will be of no avail to its union with God, as St. Paul teaches [1 Cor. 13:2]. St. Paul also says: *Charitatem habete quod est vinculum perfectionis* ("Have this charity which is the bond of perfection") [Col. 3:14]. This charity, then, causes the bridegroom to run to the spring of his bride's love, as the wounded and thirsty stag races for refreshment to the cool waters. Consequently he uses the word "cooled."

As a breeze cools and refreshes a person worn out by the heat, so this breeze of love refreshes and renews the one burning with the fire of love. The fire of love bears this property: the breeze by which it is cooled and refreshed makes it increase. For in the lover, love is a flame that burns with a desire to burn more, like the flame of natural fire. He refers to the fulfillment of this desire to burn more in his ardent love for his bride as "being cooled." In other words, he says: "In the ardor of your flight you burn more, because one love enkindles another."

It is worthy of note that God does not place his grace and love in the soul except according to its desire and love. Those truly loving God must strive not to fail in this love, for they will thereby induce God, if we may so express it, to further love them and find delight in their soul.

And to obtain this charity, the soul must practice what St. Paul taught: "Charity is patient, is kind, is not envious, does no evil, does not become proud, is not ambitious, seeks not its own, does not become disturbed, thinks no evil, rejoices not in iniquity but rejoices in the truth, suffers all things (that are to be suffered), believes all things (that must be believed), hopes all things, and endures all things (that are in accord with charity)" [1 Cor. 13:4–7].

Stanzas 14 and 15

Introduction

Since this little dove was flying in the breeze of love above the flood waters of her loving fatigues and yearnings, which she has shown until now, and could find nowhere to alight, the compassionate father Noah, stretching out his merciful hand, caught her on her last flight and placed her in the ark of his charity [Gen. 8:9]. This occurred when in the stanza we just explained the bridegroom said, "Return, dove."

Finding in this recollection all that she desired and more than is expressible, the soul begins to sing the praises of her beloved in the following stanzas. They apply to his grandeurs, which she experiences and enjoys in this union.

> My beloved, the mountains,
> And lonely wooded valleys,
> Strange islands,
> And resounding rivers,
> The whistling of love-stirring breezes,

The tranquil night
At the time of the rising dawn,
Silent music,
Sounding solitude,
The supper that refreshes, and deepens love.

Before commenting on these stanzas, we should call to mind for the sake of a clearer understanding of them, and those that follow, that this spiritual flight denotes a high state and union of love, in which, after much spiritual exercise, the soul is placed by God. This state is called spiritual espousal with the Word, the Son of God. And at the beginning, when this flight is experienced the first time, God communicates to the soul great things about himself, beautifies her with grandeur and majesty, adorns her with gifts and virtues, and clothes her with the knowledge and honor of God, as the betrothed is clothed on the day of her betrothal.

Not only do her vehement longings and complaints of love cease, but, in being graced with the blessings mentioned, a state of peace and delight and gentleness of love begins in her. This state is indicated in these stanzas, in which she does no more than tell in song her beloved's grandeurs, which she knows and enjoys in him through this union of espousal. In the remaining stanzas she no longer speaks of sufferings and longings as she did before, but of communion and exchange of sweet and peaceful love with her beloved, because now in this state all those sufferings have ceased.

It should be noted that these two stanzas describe the most that God communicates to the soul at this time. Yet it must not be thought that he communicates to all those who reach this state everything declared in these two stanzas, or that he does so in the same manner and measure of knowledge and feeling. To some souls He gives more and to others less, to some in one way and to others in another, although all alike may be in this same state of spiritual espousal. But the greatest possible communication is recorded here, because it includes everything else. The commentary follows.

Commentary on the Two Stanzas

In Noah's ark, as sacred Scripture says, there were many rooms for different kinds of animals, and all the food that could be eaten [Gen. 6:14, 19–21]. It should be noted that, similarly, the soul in her flight to the divine ark, the bosom of God, not only sees there the many dwelling places that His Majesty through St. John declared were in his Father's house [John 14:2], but sees and knows there all the foods (all the grandeurs the soul can enjoy) included in these two stanzas and signified by these common terms. These grandeurs in substance are as follows.

The soul sees and tastes abundance and inestimable riches in this divine union. She finds all the rest and recreation she desires, and understands secrets and strange knowledge of God, which is another one of the foods that taste best to her. She experiences in God an awesome power and strength which sweeps away every other power and strength. She tastes there a splendid spiritual sweetness and gratification, discovers true quiet and divine light, and tastes sublimely the wisdom of God reflected in the harmony of his creatures and works. She has the feeling of being filled with blessings and of being empty of evils and far removed from them. And above all she understands and enjoys inestimable refreshment of love, which confirms her in love. These in substance are the affirmations of the two stanzas.

The bride says in these stanzas that the beloved is all these things in himself and that he is so also for her, because in such superabundant communications from God, the soul experiences and knows the truth of St. Francis's prayer: "My God and all things." Since God is all things to the soul and the good that is in all things, the communication of this superabundance is explained through its likeness to the goodness of the things mentioned in these stanzas, which we shall explain in our commentary on each of the verses. It should be known that what is explained here is present in God eminently and infinitely, or, better, each of these sublime attributes is God, and all of them together are God.

Inasmuch as the soul in this case is united with God, she feels that all things are God, as St. John experienced when he said: *Quod factum est, in ipso vita erat* ("That which was made, had life in him") [John 1:4]. It should not be thought that what the soul is said to feel here is comparable to seeing things by means of the light, or creatures by means of God; rather, in this possession the soul feels that God is all things for her. Neither must it be thought that, because the soul has so sublime an experience of God, we are asserting that she has essential and clear vision of him. This experience is nothing but a strong and overflowing communication and glimpse of what God is in himself, in which the soul feels the goodness of the things mentioned in these verses, which we will now comment on. . . .

The whistling of love-stirring breezes. The soul refers to two things in this verse: the breezes and the whistling. By "love-stirring breezes" is understood the attributes and graces of the beloved which by means of this union assail the soul and lovingly touch it in its substance.

This most sublime and delightful knowledge of God and his attributes that overflows into the intellect from the touch these attributes of God produce in the substance of the soul she calls the whistling of these breezes. This is the most exalted delight of all the soul here enjoys.

To understand this better it should be noted that just as two things are felt in the breeze (the touch and the whistling or sound), so in this communication of the bridegroom two things are experienced: knowledge and a feeling of delight. As the feeling of the breeze delights the sense of touch, and its whistling delights the sense of hearing, so the feeling of the beloved's attributes are experienced and enjoyed by the soul's power of touch, which is in its substance, and the knowledge of these attributes is experienced in its hearing, which is its intellect.

It should also be known that the love-stirring breeze is said to come when it wounds in a pleasant way by satisfying the appetite of the one desiring such refreshment, because the sense of touch is then filled with enjoyment and refreshment; and the hearing, through the delectable touch, experiences great pleasure and gratification in the sound and whistling of the breeze. The delight of hearing is much greater than that of feeling, because the sound in the sense of hearing is more spiritual; or, better, it more closely approaches the spiritual than does feeling. Consequently, the delight of hearing is more spiritual than that of feeling.

Since this touch of God gives intense satisfaction and enjoyment to the substance of the soul, and gently fulfills her desire for this union, she calls this union, or these touches, "love-stirring breezes." As we have said, the beloved's attributes are lovingly and sweetly communicated in this breeze, and from it the intellect receives the knowledge or whistling.

She calls the knowledge a whistling, because just as the whistling of the breeze pierces deeply into the hearing organ, so this most subtle and delicate knowledge penetrates with wonderful savoriness into the innermost part of the substance of the soul, and the delight is greater than all other.

The reason for the delight is that the substance understood, stripped of its accidents and phantasms, is bestowed. For this knowledge is given to that intellect that philosophers call the passive or possible intellect, and the intellect receives it passively without any efforts of its own. This knowing is the soul's main delight, because it is pertinent to the intellect, and, as theologians say, fruition, the vision of God, is proper to the intellect.

Since this whistling refers to the substantial knowledge mentioned, some theologians think our Father Elijah saw God in that whistling of the gentle breeze heard on the mount at the mouth of his cave [1 Kings 19:11–13]. Scripture calls it the whistling of the gentle breeze, because knowledge was begotten in his intellect from the delicate spiritual communication. This knowledge is called the whistling of love-stirring breezes, because it flows over into the intellect from the loving communication of the beloved's attributes. As a result, the soul calls the knowledge the whistling of love-stirring breezes.

This divine whistling, which enters through the soul's hearing, is, as I have said, not only the substance understood, but also an unveiling of truths about the divinity and a revelation of God's secrets. When Scripture refers to a communication of God that enters by hearing, this communication ordinarily amounts to a manifestation of these naked truths to the intellect, or a revelation of the secrets of God. These are pure spiritual revelations or visions, which are given only to the spirit without the service and help of the senses. Thus what is called the communication of God through hearing is very certain and lofty. Accordingly, St. Paul, in order to declare the height of his revelation, did not say, *Vidit arcana verba* ["He saw secret words"], and still less, *Gustavit arcana verba* ["He tasted secret words"], but *Audivit arcana verba quae non licet homini loqui* ("He heard secret words which humans are not permitted to utter") [2 Cor. 12:4]. It is thought that he saw God there as our Father Elijah also did in the whistling.

Since faith, as St. Paul also says [Rom. 10:17], comes through hearing, so too that which faith tells us, the substance understood, comes through spiritual hearing. The prophet Job indicates this clearly in speaking with God, who revealed himself: *Auditu auris audivi te, nunc autem oculus meus videt te* ("With the hearing of the ear I heard you and now my eye sees you") [Job 42:5]. This passage points out clearly that to hear him with the hearing of the soul is to see Him with the eye of the passive intellect. Consequently, he does not say I heard you with the hearing of my ears, but of my ear, nor

I saw you with my eyes, but with my eye, which is the intellect. This hearing of the soul, therefore, is the vision of the intellect.

It must not be thought that, because what the soul understands is the naked substance, there is perfect and clear fruition as in heaven. Although the knowledge is stripped of accidents, it is not for this reason clear, but dark; for it is contemplation, which in this life, as St. Dionysius says, is a ray of darkness. We can say that it is a ray and image of fruition, since fruition takes place in the intellect.

This substance that is understood, and which the soul calls whistling, is equivalent to "the eyes I have desired," of which the soul said, when they were being revealed to her, "Withdraw them, beloved," because her senses could not endure them. . . .

Stanza 16

Introduction

Since the virtues of the bride are perfect and she enjoys habitual peace in the visits of her beloved, she sometimes has a sublime enjoyment of their sweetness and fragrance when her beloved touches these virtues, just as people enjoy the sweetness and beauty of flowers and lilies when they have blossomed and are handled. In many of these visits the soul sees within herself all her virtues by means of the light the bridegroom causes. And then in a wonderful delight of love she gathers them together and offers them to him as a bouquet of beautiful flowers. And he, in accepting them—for, indeed, he accepts them—receives great service.

All of this occurs interiorly. The soul feels that the beloved is within her as in his own bed. She offers herself together with her virtues, which is the greatest service she can render him. Thus one of the most remarkable delights she receives in her interior communion with God comes from this gift of herself to her beloved.

The devil, who in his great malice is envious of all the good he sees in the soul, knowing of her prosperity, now employs all his ability and engages all his crafts to disturb even a slight part of this good. It is worth more to him to hinder a small fraction of this soul's rich and glorious delight than to make many others fall into numerous serious sins, for these others have little or nothing to lose and this soul has very much to lose because of all her precious gain. The loss of a little pure gold is much worse than the loss of many other base metals.

The devil at this point takes advantage of the sensory appetites, although most of the time he can do very little or nothing, since these appetites in persons having reached this state are already deadened. When he is unable to stir these appetites, he produces a great variety of images in the imagination. He is sometimes the cause of many movements of the sensory part of the soul and of many other disturbances, spiritual as well as sensory. It is not in a person's power to be free of these until the Lord sends his angel, as is said in the psalm, round about them that fear him and delivers them [Ps. 34:7], and until he brings peace and tranquillity, both in the sensory and spiritual part of the soul.

Referring to the devil's disturbances and distrustful of the wiles he uses to cause her harm at this time, the soul, seeking this favor from God, speaks to the angels whose duty it is to assist her now by putting the devil to flight. She recites the following stanza:

> Catch us the foxes,
> For our vineyard is now in flower,
> While we fashion a cone of roses
> Intricate as the pine's;
> And let no one appear on the hill.

Commentary

Desirous that neither the envious and malicious devils, nor the wild sensory appetites, nor the various wanderings of the imagination, nor any other knowledge or awareness hamper the continuance of this interior delight of love, which is the flower of her vineyard, the bride invokes the angels, telling them to catch all these disturbances and keep them from interfering with the interior exercises of love, in the delight of which the virtues and graces are communicated and enjoyed by the soul and the Son of God. . . .

Stanza 17

Introduction

For a greater understanding of the following stanza, it should be pointed out that the absences of the beloved, which the soul suffers in this state of spiritual espousal, are very painful; some are of such a kind that there is no suffering comparable to them. The reason for such affliction is that, since she has a singular and intense love for God in this state, his absence is a singular and intense torment for her. Added to this torment is the disturbance which at this time she receives from any kind of converse or communication with creatures. Since she lives with that driving force of a fathomless desire for union with God, any delay whatever is very burdensome and disturbing, just as anything in the path of a stone which is racing on toward its center would cause in that void a violent jolt. Since the soul has already received the delight of these sweet visits, they are more desirable than gold and all beauty. Fearing as a result the great lack—even if momentary—of so precious a presence, she speaks in this stanza both to dryness and to the spirit of her bridegroom:

> Be still, deadening north wind;
> South wind come, you that waken love,
> Breathe through my garden,
> Let its fragrance flow,
> And the beloved will feed amid the flowers.

Commentary

Besides what was said in the previous stanza, spiritual dryness also hampers the interior satisfaction and sweetness of which she spoke. Dreading this, she does two things here.

First, she impedes dryness by closing the door to it through continual prayer and devotion.

Second, she invokes the Holy Spirit; it is he who will dispel this dryness and sustain and increase her love for the bridegroom. He also moves the soul to the interior exercise of the virtues, so that the Son of God, her bridegroom, may rejoice and delight more in his bride. She invokes the Holy Spirit, because her entire aim is to please her bridegroom.

Be still, deadening north wind. The north wind is very cold; it dries up and withers the flowers and plants, or at least when striking them makes them shrink and close. Because the spiritual dryness and affective absence of the beloved produces this same effect in the soul by extinguishing the satisfaction, delight, and fragrance of the virtues she was enjoying, she calls it a deadening north wind. It deadens the virtues and affective exercise, and as a result the soul pleads: "Be still, deadening north wind."

It should be understood that this plea of the soul flows from prayer and the spiritual exercises and is directed toward a detainment of the dryness. Yet since God's communications to the soul are so interior that she cannot actively move her own faculties to the enjoyment of these communications, unless the spirit of the bridegroom causes this movement of love, she invokes him saying:

South wind come, you that waken love. The south wind is a delightful breeze: it causes rain, makes the herbs and plants germinate, opens the flowers, and scatters their fragrance. Its effects are the opposite of those of the north wind. The soul, by this breeze, refers to the Holy Spirit, who awakens love. When this divine breeze strikes her, it wholly enkindles and refreshes her, and quickens and awakens the will, and elevates the previously fallen appetites that were asleep to the love of God. It does so in such a way that she can easily add "you that waken love," both his love and hers. What she asks of the Holy Spirit is expressed in the following verse:

Breathe through my garden. This garden is the soul. As the soul above calls herself a vineyard in flower, because the flowers of the virtues within her supply sweet-tasting wine, here she calls herself a garden, because the flowers of perfections and virtues planted within her come to life and begin to grow.

It should be noted that the bride does not say "Breathe into my garden," but "Breathe through my garden," for there is a considerable difference between God's breathing into the soul and his breathing through the soul. To breathe into the soul is to infuse graces, gifts, and virtues. To breathe through the soul is to touch and put in motion the virtues and perfections already given, renewing and moving them in such a way that they of themselves afford the soul a wonderful fragrance and sweetness, as when you shake aromatic spices and they spread their abundant fragrance, which prior to this was neither so strong nor so highly perceptible. The soul is not always experiencing and enjoying the acquired or infused virtues actually, because, as we shall see later, they remain within her in this life like flowers enclosed in the bud or like aromatic spices whose scent is not perceived until shaken and uncovered.

God sometimes grants these favors to the soul, his bride. He breathes through her flowering garden, opens all these buds of virtues, and uncovers these aromatic spices of gifts, perfections, and riches; and, disclosing this interior treasure and wealth, he reveals all her beauty. And then it is something wonderful to behold and pleasant to feel: the wealth of her gifts unveiled to the soul and the beauty of these flowers of virtues now in full bloom. And the fragrant scent each one, with its own characteristics, gives to her is inestimable. . . .

Stanzas 20 and 21

Introduction

The attainment of so high a state of perfection as that which the soul here aims after, which is spiritual marriage, requires the purification of all the imperfections, rebellions, and imperfect habits of the lower part, which, by putting off the old self, is surrendered and made subject to the higher part; but there is also needed a singular fortitude and a very sublime love for so strong and intimate an embrace from God. The soul obtains not only a very lofty purity and beauty, but also an amazing strength because of the powerful and intimate bond effected between God and her by means of this union.

In order that she reach him, it is necessary for her to attain an adequate degree of purity, fortitude, and love. The Holy Spirit, he who intervenes to effect this spiritual union, desiring that the soul attain the possession of these qualities in order to merit this union, speaks to the Father and the Son in the Canticle: "What shall we do for our sister on the day of her courtship, for she is little and has no breasts? If she is a wall, let us build upon it silver bulwarks and defenses; and if she is a door, let us reinforce it with cedar wood" [Song of Sol. 8:8–9]. The silver bulwarks and defenses refer to the strong and heroic virtues clothed with faith, which is signified by silver. These heroic virtues are those of spiritual marriage, and their foundation is in the strong soul, referred to by the wall. The peaceful bridegroom rests in the strength of these virtues without any weakness disturbing him. The cedar wood applies to the affections and properties of lofty love. This lofty love is signified by cedar, and it is the love proper to spiritual marriage. The bride must first be a door in order to receive the reinforcement of cedar wood; that is, she must hold the door of her will open to the bridegroom that he may enter through the complete and true yes of love. This is the yes of espousal, which is given before the spiritual marriage. The breasts of the bride also refer to this perfect love that she should possess in order to appear before the bridegroom, Christ, for the consummation of this state.

The text, however, mentions that the bride answered immediately by stating her desire to be courted: "I am a wall and my breasts are as a tower" [Song of Sol. 8:10]. This means: "My soul is strong and my love lofty, and so I should not be held back." Desiring this perfect union and transformation, the bride also manifested this strength in the preceding stanzas, especially in the one just explained, in which to oblige her spouse further she sets before him the virtues and preparative riches received from him. As a result the bridegroom, desiring to conclude this matter, speaks the two following stanzas, in which he finishes purifying the soul, strengthening and disposing her in both sensory and spiritual parts for this state. He speaks these lines against all the oppositions and rebellions from the sensory part and the devil.

Swift-winged birds,
Lions, stags, and leaping roes,
Mountains, lowlands, and river banks,
Waters, winds, and ardors,
Watching fears of night:

By the pleasant lyres
And the siren's song, I conjure you
To cease your anger
And not touch the wall,
That the bride may sleep in deeper peace. . . .

Stanza 22

Introduction

Great was the desire of the bridegroom to free and ransom his
bride completely from the hands of sensuality and the devil.
Like the good shepherd rejoicing and holding on his shoulders
the lost sheep for which he had searched along many winding
paths [Luke 15:4–5], and like the woman who, having lit the
candle and hunted through her whole house for the lost
drachma, holding it up in her hands with gladness and calling
to her friends and neighbors to come and celebrate, saying,
rejoice with me, and so on [Luke 15:8–9], now, too, that the
soul is liberated, this loving shepherd and bridegroom rejoices.
And it is wonderful to see his pleasure in carrying the rescued,
perfected soul on his shoulders, held there by his hands in this
desired union.

Not only does he himself rejoice, but he also makes the angels and saintly souls share in his gladness, saying in the words of the Song of Songs: "Go forth daughters of Zion and behold King Solomon in the crown with which his mother crowned him on the day of his espousal and on the day of the joy of his heart" [Song of Sol. 3:11]. By these words he calls the soul his crown, his bride, and the joy of his heart, and he takes her now in his arms and goes forth with her as the bridegroom from his bridal chamber [Ps. 19:5]. He refers to this in the following stanza:

> The bride has entered
> The sweet garden of her desire,
> And she rests in delight,
> Laying her neck
> On the gentle arms of her beloved.

Commentary

Now that the bride has diligently sought to catch the foxes, still the north wind, and calm the girls of Judea, all of which are obstacles to the full delight of the state of spiritual marriage; and now that she has also invoked and obtained the breeze of the Holy Spirit, as in the preceding stanzas, which entails the proper preparation and the instrument for the perfection of this state, we must treat this state by explaining the stanza. Here the bridegroom speaks and, in calling the soul "bride," declares two things.

First, he tells how, now victorious, she has reached this pleasant state of spiritual marriage, which was his as well as her ardent longing.

And second, he enumerates the properties of this state that the soul now enjoys, such as: resting in delight and laying her neck on the gentle arms of her beloved, as we will explain.

The bride has entered. To offer a more lucid explanation of the order of these stanzas and of what the soul usually passes through before reaching this state of spiritual marriage, which is the highest (that which, with the divine help, we will now speak of), it should be noted that before the soul reaches this state she first exercises herself both in the trials and the bitterness of mortification and in meditation on spiritual things. This is referred to from the first stanza until that which says: "Pouring out a thousand graces." Afterward she embarks on the contemplative way. Here she passes along the paths and straits of love about which she sings in the sequence of the verses until that stanza which begins, "Withdraw them, beloved," where the spiritual espousal is wrought. Afterward, she advances along the unitive way, in which she receives many remarkable communications, visits, gifts, and jewels from her bridegroom and, as one betrothed, learns of her beloved and becomes perfect in loving him; this she relates starting at the stanza in which the espousal was made ("Withdraw them, beloved") until this one beginning with, "The bride has entered," where the spiritual marriage between the soul and the Son of God is effected.

This spiritual marriage is incomparably greater than the spiritual espousal, for it is a total transformation in the beloved in which each surrenders the entire possession of self to the other with a certain consummation of the union of love. The soul thereby becomes divine, becomes God through participation, insofar as is possible in this life. And thus I think that this state never occurs without the soul's being confirmed in grace, for the faith of both is confirmed when God's faith in the soul is here confirmed. It is accordingly the highest state attainable in this life.

Just as in the consummation of carnal marriage there are two in one flesh, as sacred Scripture points out [Gen. 2:24], so also when the spiritual marriage between God and the soul is consummated, there are two natures in one spirit and love, as St. Paul says in making this same comparison: "Whoever is joined to the Lord is one spirit with him" [1 Cor. 6:17]. This union resembles the union of the light of a star or candle with the light of the sun, for what then sheds light is not the star or the candle, but the sun, which has absorbed the other lights into its own.

The bridegroom speaks of the state in this verse, saying the bride has entered, that is, she has entered, leaving behind everything temporal and natural and all spiritual affections, modes, and manners, and has set aside and forgotten all temptations, disturbances, pains, solicitude, and cares, and is transformed in this high embrace. The next line follows:

The sweet garden of her desire. This is like saying she has been transformed into her God, here referred to as "the sweet garden," because of the sweet and pleasant dwelling she finds in him. One does not reach this garden of full transformation, which is the joy, delight, and glory of spiritual marriage, without first passing through the spiritual espousal and the loyal and mutual love of betrothed persons. For after the soul has been for some time the betrothed of the Son of God in gentle and complete love, God calls her and places her in his flowering garden to consummate this most joyful state of marriage with him. The union wrought between the two natures and the communication of the divine to the human in this state is such that even though neither changes its being, both appear to be God. Yet in this life the union cannot be perfect, although it is beyond words and thought.

The bridegroom points this out clearly in the Song of Songs where he invites the soul, now his betrothed, to this state: *Veni in hortum meum, soror mea sponsa, messui myrrham meam cum aromatibus meis* ("Come and enter my garden, my sister, my bride, for now I have gathered my myrrh with my fragrant spices") [Song of Sol. 5:1]. He calls her sister and bride because she was a sister and bride in the love and surrender she had made of herself to him before he called her to this state of spiritual marriage, where, as he says, he has now gathered his fragrant myrrh and aromatic spices, which are the fruits of the flowers now ripe and ready for the soul. These are the delights and grandeurs that of himself and in himself he communicates to her in this state.

Consequently he is for her an enchanting, desirable garden, for her entire aim in all her works is the consummation and perfection of this state. She never rests until reaching it. She finds in this state a much greater abundance and fullness of God, a more secure and stable peace, and an incomparably more perfect delight than in the spiritual espousal; here it is as though she were placed in the arms of her bridegroom. As a result she usually experiences an intimate spiritual embrace, which is a veritable embrace, by means of which she lives the life of God. The words of St. Paul are verified in this soul: "I live, now not I, but Christ lives in me" [Gal. 2:20].

Wherefore, since the soul lives in this state a life as happy and glorious as is God's, let each one consider here, if possible, how pleasant her life is. Just as God is incapable of feeling any distaste neither does she feel any, for the delight of God's glory is experienced and enjoyed in the substance of the soul now transformed in him.

As a result the next verse continues:

> And she rests in delight,
> Laying her neck

The neck refers here to the soul's strength by means of which, as we said, is effected this union with her bridegroom, because she would be unable to endure so intimate an embrace if she were not now very strong. And because the soul labored, it is right that with the strength by which she struggled and conquered she repose, laying her neck

On the gentle arms of her beloved. To recline her neck on the arms of God is to have her strength, or, better, her weakness, now united to the strength of God, for the arms signify God's strength. Accordingly this state of spiritual marriage is very aptly designated by the laying of her neck on the gentle arms of the beloved, for now God is the soul's strength and sweetness, in which she is sheltered and protected against all evils and habituated to the delight of all goods.

Desirous of this state, the bride spoke to the bridegroom in the Song of Songs: "Who will give you to me for my brother, nursed at the breasts of my mother, that I may find you alone outside and kiss you, and no one despise me?" [Song of Sol. 8:1]. In calling him brother, she indicates the equality of love between the two in the espousal before this state is reached. And in saying, "nursed at the breasts of my mother," she means: "You dried up and subdued in me the appetites and passions, which in our flesh are the breasts and milk of mother Eve, and an impediment to this state. And when this is accomplished 'that I may find you alone outside,' that is, outside of all things and of myself, in solitude and nakedness of spirit, which is attained when the appetites are dried up. And alone there, 'kiss you' alone, that is, that my nature, now alone and denuded of all temporal, natural, and spiritual impurity, may be united with you alone, with your nature alone, through no intermediary." This union is found only in the spiritual marriage, in which the soul kisses God without contempt or disturbance from anyone. For in this state neither the flesh, nor the world, nor the devil molest her, nor do the appetites. Here we find also the fulfillment of what is said in the Song of Songs: "Winter is now past, the rain is gone, and the flowers have appeared in our land" [Song of Sol. 2:11–12].

Stanza 23

Introduction

In this high state of spiritual marriage the bridegroom reveals his wonderful secrets to the soul, as to his faithful consort, with remarkable ease and frequency, for true and perfect love knows not how to keep anything hidden from the beloved. He communicates to her, mainly, sweet mysteries of his Incarnation and of the ways of the redemption of humanity, which is one of the loftiest of his works, and thus more delightful to the soul. Even though he communicates many other mysteries to her, the bridegroom in the following stanza mentions only the Incarnation, as the most important. In speaking to the soul he says:

> Beneath the apple tree:
> There I took you for my own,
> There I offered you my hand,
> And restored you,
> Where your mother was corrupted.

Commentary

The bridegroom explains to the soul in this stanza his admirable plan in redeeming and espousing her to himself through the very means by which human nature was corrupted and ruined, telling her that as human nature through Adam was ruined and corrupted by means of the forbidden tree in the garden of Paradise, so on the tree of the cross it was redeemed and restored when he gave it there, through his passion and death, the hand of his favor and mercy, and broke down the barriers between God and humans, which were built up through original sin. Thus he says:

Beneath the apple tree. That is: beneath the favor of the tree of the cross (referred to by the apple tree), where the Son of God redeemed human nature and consequently espoused it to himself, and then espoused each soul by giving it through the cross grace and pledges for this espousal. And thus he says:

> There I took you for my own,
> There I offered you my hand.

That is: "There I offered you my kind regard and help by raising you from your low state to be my companion and spouse."

> And restored you,
> Where your mother was corrupted.

"For human nature, your mother, was corrupted in your first parents, under the tree, and you too under the tree of the cross were restored. If your mother, therefore, brought you death under the tree, I, under the tree of the cross, brought you life." In such a way God manifests the decrees of his wisdom; he knows how to draw good from evil so wisely and beautifully, and to ordain to a greater good what was a cause of evil.

The bridegroom himself literally speaks this stanza to the bride in the Song of Songs: *Sub arbore malo suscitavi te; ibi corrupta est mater tua, ibi violata est genetrix tua* ("Under the apple tree I raised you up; there your mother was corrupted, there she who bore you was violated") [Song of Sol. 8:5].

The espousal made on the cross is not the one we now speak of. For that espousal is accomplished immediately when God gives the first grace, which is bestowed on each one at baptism. The espousal of which we speak bears reference to perfection and is not achieved save gradually and by stages. For though it is all one espousal, there is a difference in that one is attained at the soul's pace, and thus little by little, and the other at God's pace, and thus immediately. . . .

Stanza 26

Introduction

What, then, is the state of this happy soul in her bed of flowers, where these things and so many others take place, in which she has for her couch the bridegroom, the Son of God, and love of this very bridegroom for a covering and hanging? She can certainly repeat the words of the bride: "His left hand is under my head" [Song of Sol. 2:6]. We can therefore assert truly that this soul is here clothed with God and bathed in divinity, not as though on the surface, but in the interior of her spirit, superabounding in divine delights. In the fullness of the spiritual waters of life, she experiences what David says of those who have reached God: "They shall be inebriated with the plenty of your house; and you will give them to drink of the torrent of your delight, because with you is the fountain of life" [Ps. 36:8–9]. What fulfillment will the soul have in her being, since the drink given her is no less than a torrent of delight! This torrent is the Holy Spirit because, as St. John says, "He is a resplendent river of living water that flows from the throne of God and of the Lamb" [Rev. 22:1]. These waters, since they are the intimate love of God, flow intimately into the soul and give her to drink of this torrent of love, which, as we said, is the Spirit of her bridegroom infused in this union. As a result she sings this stanza with abundant love:

> In the inner wine cellar
> I drank of my beloved, and when I went abroad

> Through all this valley
> I no longer knew anything,
> And lost the herd that I was following. . . .

Commentary

I no longer knew anything. The reason is that the drink of highest wisdom makes her forget all worldly things. And it seems that her previous knowledge, and even all the knowledge of the world, in comparison with this knowledge is pure ignorance.

For a better understanding of this, it should be known that the most formal cause of the soul's knowing nothing of the world when in this state is that she is being informed with supernatural knowledge, in the presence of which all natural and political knowledge of the world is ignorance rather than knowledge. When the soul is brought into this lofty knowing, she understands by means of it that all other knowledge that has not the taste of this knowledge is not knowledge but ignorance, and that there is nothing to know in it. She declares the truth of the Apostle's words, that what is greater wisdom in the sight of humans is foolishness before God [1 Cor. 3:19]. Hence she asserts that after drinking of that divine wisdom she no longer knew anything.

And this truth (that human wisdom and that of the whole world is pure ignorance and unworthy of being known) cannot be understood except by this favor of God's presence in the soul, by which he communicates his wisdom and comforts her with the drink of love that she may behold this truth clearly, as Solomon explains: "This is the vision that the man who is with God saw and spoke. And being comforted by God's dwelling within him, he said: I am the most foolish among humans, and human wisdom is not with me" [Prov. 30:1–2].

The reason is that in the excess of the lofty wisdom of God lowly human wisdom is ignorance. The natural sciences themselves and the very works of God, when set beside what it is to know God, are like ignorance. For where God is unknown nothing is known. The high things of God are foolishness and madness to humans, as St. Paul says [1 Cor. 2:14]. Hence the wise people of God and the wise people of the world are foolish in the eyes of each other, for the one group finds the wisdom and knowledge of God imperceptible, and the other finds the same of the knowledge of the world. Wherefore the knowledge of the world is ignorance to the knowledge of God, and the knowledge of God is ignorance to the knowledge of the world.

On the other hand, that elevation and immersion of the mind in God, in which the soul is as though carried away and absorbed in love, entirely transformed in God, does not allow attention to any worldly thing. She is not only annihilated before all things and estranged from them, but even from herself, as if she had vanished and been dissolved in love; all of which consists in passing out of self to the beloved. Thus the bride in the Song of Songs, after having treated the transformation of her love into the beloved, refers to this unknowing, in which she was left, by the word nescivi ("I did not know") [Song of Sol. 6:12].

In a way, the soul in this state resembles Adam in the state of innocence, who did not know evil. For she is so innocent that she does not understand evil, nor does she judge anything in a bad light.

And she will hear very evil things and see them with her own eyes and be unable to understand that they are so, since she does not have within herself the habit of evil by which to judge them; for God by means of the perfect habit of true wisdom has destroyed her habitual imperfections and ignorances, which include the evil of sin.

And so too in regard to her words "I no longer knew anything," she takes little part in the affairs of others, for she is not even mindful of her own. This is a characteristic of God's spirit in the soul: he gives her an immediate inclination toward ignoring and not desiring knowledge of the affairs of others, especially that which brings her no benefit. God's spirit is turned toward the soul to draw her away from external affairs rather than involve her in them. Thus she remains in an unknowing, in the manner she was accustomed to.

It should not be thought that because she remains in this unknowing that she loses there her acquired knowledge of the sciences; rather, these habits are perfected by the more perfect habit of supernatural knowledge infused in her. Yet these habits do not reign in such a way that she must use them in order to know; though at times she may still use them since this supernatural knowledge does not impede their use. For in this union with divine wisdom these habits are joined to the superior wisdom of God. When a faint light is mingled with a bright one, the bright light prevails and is that which illumines. Yet the faint light is not lost, but rather perfected, even though it is not the light that illumines principally.

Such, I believe, will be the case in heaven. The habits of knowledge that were acquired by the just will not be supplanted, but they will not be of great benefit either, since the just will have more knowledge through the divine wisdom than through these habits.

Yet particular knowledge, forms of things, imaginative acts, and any other apprehensions involving form and figure are all lost and ignored in that absorption of love. There are two reasons for this.

First, since the soul is absorbed and imbibed in that drink of love, she cannot advert actually to any other thing.

Second, and principally, that transformation in God makes her so consonant with the simplicity and purity of God, in which there is no form or imaginative figure, that it leaves her clean, pure, and empty of all forms and figures, purged, and radiant in simple contemplation. The effect of this contemplation is like that of the sun on a window. In shining on the window, the sun makes it look bright, and all the stains and smudges previously apparent are lost sight of; yet when the sunlight passes, the stains and smudges reappear.

Since the effect of that act of love endures a while, the unknowing also continues, so that the soul cannot advert to anything in particular until the effect of that act of love passes. Since that act of love inflamed and transformed her into love, it annihilated her and did away with all that was not love, as is understood in what we mentioned above concerning David: "Because my heart was inflamed, my reins were also changed, and I was brought to nothing and knew not" [Ps. 73:21–22]. The change of the reins because of this inflammation of the heart is a change of the soul, according to her operations and appetites, into God, into a new kind of life in which she is undone and annihilated before all the old things she formerly made use of. The prophet thus says that he was brought to nothing and did not know, for these are the two effects we mentioned of this drink from the wine cellar of God. . . .

Stanza 27

Introduction

In this interior union God communicates himself to the soul with such genuine love that no mother's affection, in which she tenderly caresses her child, no brother's love, nor friendship is comparable to it. The tenderness and truth of love by which the immense Father favors and exalts this humble and loving soul reaches such a degree—O wonderful thing, worthy of all our awe and admiration—that the Father himself becomes subject to her for her exaltation, as though he were her servant and she his lord. And he is as solicitous in favoring her as he would be if he were her slave and she his god. So profound is the humility and sweetness of God!

In this communication of love, he exercises in some way that very service that he says in the gospel he will render to his elect in heaven, that is: girding himself and passing from one to another, he will minister to them [Luke 12:37]. He is occupied here in favoring and caressing the soul like a mother who ministers to her child and nurses it at her own breasts. The soul thereby comes to know the truth of Isaiah's words: "You shall be carried at the breast of God and upon his knees you will be caressed" [Isa. 66:12].

What then will be the soul's experience among such sovereign graces! How she will be dissolved in love! How thankful she will be to see the breasts of God given to her with such supreme and generous love! Aware that she has been set among so many delights, she makes a complete surrender of herself and gives him the breast of her will and love. She experiences this surrender of her soul in the way the bride did in the Canticle when speaking to her bridegroom: "I turn to my beloved, and his turning is toward me. Come my beloved, let us go into the field, let us abide together on the grange; let us rise very early and go to the vine-yards to see if the vine is in flower and if the flowers bear fruit, if the pomegranates flourish; there will I give you my breasts" (that is, "I shall employ the delights and strength of my will in your love") [Song of Sol. 7:11–12]. . . .

Stanza 28

Introduction

Because we said that God makes use of nothing other than love, it may prove beneficial to explain the reason for this, prior to commenting on the stanza. The reason is that all our works and our trials, even though they are the greatest possible, are nothing in the sight of God. For through them we cannot give him anything or fulfill his only desire, which is the exaltation of the soul. Of these other things he desires nothing for himself, since he has no need of them. If anything pleases him, it is the exaltation of the soul. Since there is no way by which he can exalt her more than by making her equal to himself, he is pleased only with her love. For the property of love is to make the lover equal to the object loved. Since the soul in this state possesses perfect love, she is called the bride of the Son of God, which signifies equality with him. In this equality of friendship the possessions of both are held in common, as the bridegroom himself said to his disciples: "I have now called you my friends because all that I have heard from my Father I have manifested to you" [John 15:15].

   She then recites the stanza:

> Now I occupy my soul
> And all my energy in his service;
> I no longer tend the herd,
> Nor have I any other work
> Now that my every act is love.

Commentary

Since in the last stanza the soul—or, better, the bride—said she surrendered herself entirely to the bridegroom without keeping anything back, she now tells of her mode and method in accomplishing this, saying that now she occupies her soul and body, her faculties and all her ability, in nothing other than the service of her bridegroom. And she says that on this account she no longer goes about in search of her own gain or pleasures, nor occupies herself with things and matters foreign to God; and that even with God himself she has no other style or manner of dealing than the exercise of love, since she has now traded and changed for love all her first manner of dealing with him, as is now said:

Now I occupy my soul. By saying that she occupies her soul, she refers to her surrender to the beloved in that union of love where now the soul and all the faculties (intellect, memory, and will) are dedicated and devoted to his service. She employs the intellect in understanding and carrying out the things that are more for his service, and the will in loving all that is pleasing to him and attaching it to him in all things, and her memory and care in what most pleases and serves him. And she adds:

And all my energy in his service. By "all her energy" she refers to all that pertains to the sensory part of the soul. The sensory part includes the body with all its senses and faculties, interior and exterior, and all the natural ability (the four passions, the natural appetites, and other energies).

All of this, she says, she occupies, as she does the rational and spiritual part referred to in the preceding verse, in the service of her beloved. By directing the activity of the interior and exterior senses toward God, her use of the body is now conformed to his will. She also binds the four passions of the soul to him, for she does not rejoice except in God, nor hope in anything other than God; she fears only God and has no sorrow unless in relation to him. And likewise all her appetites and cares go out only to God.

All this energy is occupied in God, and so directed to him that even without advertence all its parts, which we have mentioned, are inclined from their first movements to work in and for God. The intellect, will, and memory go out immediately toward God, and the affections, senses, desires, appetites, hope, joy, and all the energy from the first instant incline toward God, although, as I say, the soul may not advert to the fact that she is working for him.

As a result she frequently works for God, and is occupied in him and in his affairs without thinking or being aware that she is doing so. For her custom and habit of acting in this way causes her to lack advertence and care and even the fervent acts she used to make in beginning some work.

Because this energy is now all employed in God, the soul necessarily achieves the condition described in the following verse:

I no longer tend the herd. This is like saying: "I no longer follow after my pleasures and appetites." For having placed them in God and given them to him, she no longer feeds them or keeps them for herself. She does not merely say she no longer tends this herd, but even more:

Nor have I any other work. Before reaching this gift and surrender of herself and her energy to the beloved, the soul usually has many unprofitable occupations, by which she endeavors to serve her own appetite and that of others. For we can say she had as much work as she had many habitual imperfections. These habitual imperfections can be, for example, the trait or "work" of speaking about useless things, thinking about them, and also carrying them out, or of not making use of these actions in accord with the demands of perfection. She usually has desires to serve the appetites of others, which she does through ostentatiousness, compliments, flattery, human respect, the effort to impress and please people by her actions, and many other useless things. In this fashion she strives to satisfy people, employing for them all her care, desires, work, and finally energy.

She says she no longer has all this work, because all her words, thoughts, and works are of God and directed toward him without any of the former imperfections. Thus the verse means: "I no longer tend to giving satisfaction to my appetite or that of others, neither am I occupied or detained with other useless pastimes or things of the world."

Now that my every act is love. This is like saying that now all this work is directed to the practice of love of God, that is: "All the ability of my soul and body (memory, intellect, and will, interior and exterior senses, appetites of the sensory and spiritual part) moves in love and because of love. Everything I do, I do with love, and everything I suffer, I suffer with the delight of love." David meant this when he said: "I shall keep my strength for you" [Ps. 59:9].

It should be known that when the soul reaches this state, all the activity of the spiritual and sensory part (in which it does, or in what it suffers, and in whatever manner) always causes more love and delight in God, as we have said. Even the very exercise of prayer and communion with God, in which she was accustomed to considerations and methods, is now wholly the exercise of love. Hence whether her work is temporal or spiritual, this soul can always say, "Now that my every act is love."

Happy is the life and state, and happy the person who attains it, where everything is now the substance of love and the pleasure and delight of espousal. The bride in this state can indeed say to the divine bridegroom those words she spoke to him out of pure love in the Song of Songs: "All the new and old apples I have kept for you" [Song of Sol. 7:13], which is equivalent to saying: "My beloved, all that is rough and toilsome I desire for your sake, and all that is sweet and pleasant I desire for your sake." Yet the accommodated sense of this verse is that the soul in this state of spiritual espousal ordinarily walks in the union of love of God, which is a habitual and loving attentiveness of the will to God.

Stanza 29

Introduction

This soul, indeed, lost to all things and won over to love, no longer occupies her spirit in anything else. She even withdraws in matters pertinent to the active life and exterior occupations for the sake of fulfilling the one thing the bridegroom said was necessary [Luke 10:42], and that is: attentiveness to God and continual love of him. This the Lord values and esteems so highly that he reproved Martha when she tried to call Mary away from her place at his feet in order to busy her with other active things in his service. And Martha thought that she herself was doing all the work and that Mary, because she was enjoying the Lord's presence, was doing nothing [Luke 10:39–41]. Yet, since there is no greater or more necessary work than love, the contrary is true. He also defends the bride in the Song of Songs, conjuring all creatures of the world, referred to by the daughters of Jerusalem, not to hinder the bride's spiritual sleep of love or cause her to awaken or open her eyes to anything else until she desires [Song of Sol. 3:5].

It should be noted that until the soul reaches this state of union of love, she should practice love in both the active and contemplative life. Yet once she arrives, she should not become involved in other works and exterior exercises that might be of the slightest hindrance to the attentiveness of love toward God, even though the work be of great service to God. For a little of this pure love is more precious to God and the soul and more beneficial to the church, even though it seems one is doing nothing, than all these other works put together.

Because of her determined desire to please her spouse and benefit the church, Mary Magdalene, even though she was accomplishing great good by her preaching and would have continued doing so, hid in the desert for thirty years in order to surrender herself truly to this love. It seemed to her, after all, that by such retirement she would obtain much more because of the notable benefit and gain a little of this love brings to the church.

Great wrong would be done to those who possess some degree of this solitary love, as well as to the church, if we should urge them to become occupied in exterior or active things, even if the works are very important and demand only a short time. Since God has solemnly entreated that no one awaken a soul from this love [Song of Sol. 3:5], who will dare do so and remain without reproof? After all, this love is the end for which we were created.

Let those, then, who are singularly active, who think they can win the world with their preaching and exterior works, observe here that they would profit the church and please God much more, not to mention the good example they would give, were they to spend at least half of this time with God in prayer, even though they may not have reached a prayer as sublime as this. They would then certainly accomplish more, and with less labor, by one work than they otherwise would by a thousand. For through their prayer they would merit this result, and themselves be spiritually strengthened. Without prayer they would do a great deal of hammering but accomplish little, and sometimes nothing, and even at times cause harm.

God forbid that the salt should begin to lose its savor [Matt. 5:13], for however much they may appear to achieve externally, they will in substance be accomplishing nothing; it is beyond doubt that good works can be performed only by the power of God.

Oh, how much could be written here on this subject! But this is not the place. I have mentioned it only in explanation of the next stanza. In this stanza the soul replies to all those who impugn her holy idleness, and who desire every work to be the kind that shines outwardly and satisfies the eye, and do not know the secret source from which the water flows and all fruit is produced.

And thus she recites the stanza:

> If, then, I am no longer
> Seen or found on the common,
> You will say that I am lost;
> That, stricken by love,
> I lost myself, and was found.

Commentary

In this stanza the soul answers a tacit reproof of those in the world who usually criticize persons who are entirely given to God and think these persons excessive in their conduct, estrangement, and withdrawal, and assert that they are useless in important matters and lost to what the world esteems. The soul skillfully answers this reprimand, boldly facing it and all the other possible reproofs of the world; for in having reached the intimate love of God, she considers everything else of little consequence.

But this is not all. She even proclaims how she has acted, and rejoices and glories in having lost the world and herself for her beloved. This is what she means in the stanza when she addresses the worldly: that, if they no longer see her engaged in her former worldly conversations and pastimes, they should believe and declare that she has lost these things and withdrawn; and that she has counted this loss such a good that she herself, searching for her beloved and intensely enamored of him, desired it. That they might see the gain of her loss and not think it an absurdity or a delusion, she declares that her loss was her gain, and that as a result she became lost purposely.

> If, then, I am no longer
> Seen or found on the common

The place where people often gather for diversion and recreation, and where shepherds also feed their flocks, is usually called the common. Thus, by the common the soul refers to the world, where worldlings engage in their pastimes and conversations and feed the flock of their appetites. In this verse she tells those who are of the world that if they neither see nor find her as they did before her complete surrender to God, they should consider her, by this fact, lost, and they should therefore say (because she rejoices in their saying this and desires them to do so):

You will say that I am lost. Those who love are not abashed before the world because of the works they perform for God; nor even if everybody condemns them do they hide them in shame. Those who are ashamed to confess the Son of God before others, by failing to perform his works, will discover that the Son of God, as is recorded in Luke, will be ashamed to confess them before the Father [Luke 9:26]. The soul possessing the spirit of love glories, rather, in beholding that she has achieved this work in praise of her beloved and lost all things of the world. Hence she says: "You will say that I am lost."

Few spiritual persons reach such daring and determination in their works. Though some do act this way and are considered far advanced, they never lose themselves entirely in some matters, whether worldly or natural, and never execute works for Christ with perfection and nakedness of spirit and without thought of what others will say or how their work will appear. Since these persons are not lost to themselves in their work, they cannot declare: "You will say that I am lost." They are still ashamed to confess Christ before others by their works. Because of their human respect they do not live entirely in Christ.

That, stricken by love. This means that, through the practice of virtue, stricken with love, [she lost herself, and was found].

I lost myself, and was found. Aware of the bridegroom's words in the gospel, that no one can serve two masters, but must necessarily fail one [Matt. 6:24], the soul claims here that in order not to fail God, she failed all that is not God, that is, herself and all other creatures, losing all these for love of him. Those who truly walk in love let themselves lose all things immediately in order to be found more attached to what they love. On this account the soul affirms here that she lost herself. She achieved this in two ways: she became lost to herself by paying no attention to herself in anything, by concentrating on her beloved and surrendering herself to him freely and disinterestedly, with no desire to gain anything for herself; second, she became lost to all creatures, paying no heed to all her own affairs, but only to those of her beloved. And this is to lose herself purposely, which is to desire to be found.

Those who walk in the love of God seek neither their own gain nor their reward, but only to lose all things and themselves for God; and this loss they judge to be their gain. And thus it is as St. Paul asserts: Mori lucrum [Phil. 1:21], that is, my death for Christ is the spiritual gain of all things and of myself. And consequently the soul declares, "I was found." Those who do not know how to lose themselves do not find themselves, but rather lose themselves, as our Lord teaches in the gospels: "Those who desire to gain their soul shall lose it, and those who lose it for my sake shall gain it" [Matt. 16:25].

Should we desire to interpret this verse more spiritually and in closer accord with what we are discussing here, it ought to be known that when a soul treading the spiritual road has reached such a point that she has lost all roads and natural methods in her communion with God, and no longer seeks him by reflections, or forms, or sentiments, or by any other way of creatures and the senses, but has advanced beyond them all and beyond all modes and manners, and enjoys communion with God in faith and love, then it is said that God is her gain, because she has certainly lost all that is not God. . . .

Stanza 36

Introduction

Strange it is, this property of lovers, that they like to enjoy each other's companionship alone, apart from every creature and all company. If some stranger is present, they do not enjoy each other freely, even though they are together and may speak to each other just as much when the other is present as when absent, and even though this stranger does not talk to them. The reason they desire to commune with each other alone is that love is a union between two alone. . . .

> Let us rejoice, beloved,
> And let us go forth to behold ourselves in your beauty,
> To the mountain and to the hill,
> To where the pure water flows,
> And further, deep into the thicket. . . .

Commentary

Let us rejoice, beloved. That is: "Let us rejoice in the communication of the sweetness of love, not only in that sweetness we already possess in our habitual union, but in that which overflows into the effective and actual practice of love, either interiorly with the will in the affective act, or exteriorly in works directed to the service of the beloved." As we mentioned, when love takes root it has this characteristic: it makes one always desire to taste its joys and sweetnesses, which are the inward and outward exercise of love. All this the lover does in order to resemble the beloved more. And thus she continues:

And let us go forth to behold ourselves in your beauty. This means: "Let us so act that by means of this loving activity we may attain to the vision of ourselves in your beauty in eternal life." That is: "That I may be so transformed in your beauty that we may be alike in beauty, and both behold ourselves in your beauty, possessing now your very beauty; this, in such a way that looking at each other we may see in each other our own beauty, since both of us are your beauty alone, I being absorbed in your beauty; hence, I shall see you in your beauty, and you shall see me in your beauty, and I shall see myself in you in your beauty, and you will see yourself in me in your beauty; that I may resemble you in your beauty, and you resemble me in your beauty, and my beauty be your beauty and your beauty be my beauty; wherefore I shall be you in your beauty, and you will be me in your beauty, because your very beauty will be my beauty; and therefore we shall behold each other in your beauty."

This is the adoption of the children of God, who will indeed declare to God what the very Son said to the Eternal Father through St. John: "All my things are yours, and yours mine" [John 17:10]. He says this by essence, since he is the natural Son of God, and we say it by participation, since we are adopted children. He declared this not only for himself, the head, but for his whole mystical body, the church, which on the day of her triumph, when she sees God face to face, will participate in the very beauty of the bridegroom. Hence the soul makes the petition that she and her bridegroom go forth to behold each other in his beauty. . . .

Stanza 37

Introduction

One of the main reasons for the desire to be dissolved and to be with Christ [Phil. 1:23] is to see him face to face and thoroughly understand the profound and eternal mysteries of his Incarnation, which is by no means the lesser part of beatitude. As Christ himself says to the Father in St. John's gospel: "This is eternal life that they might know you, the one true God, and your Son Jesus Christ whom you have sent" [John 17:3]. The first thing a person desires to do after having come a long distance is to see and converse with the one deeply loved. Similarly, the first thing the soul desires on coming to the vision of God is to know and enjoy the deep secrets and mysteries of the Incarnation and the ancient ways of God dependent on it. Hence after expressing her desire to see herself in the beauty of God, the soul declares in the following stanza:

> And then we will go on
> To the high caverns in the rock
> Which are so well concealed;
> There we shall enter
> And taste the fresh juice of the pomegranates.

Commentary

One of the reasons urging the soul most to enter this thicket of God's wisdom and know its beauty from further within is her wish to unite her intellect with God in the knowledge of the mysteries of the Incarnation, in which is contained the highest and most savory wisdom of all his works. The bride states in this stanza that once she has entered further into the divine wisdom (further into the spiritual marriage she now possesses, which will be the face-to-face vision of God in glory as well as union with the divine wisdom, who is the Son of God), she will know the sublime mysteries of God and of humanity. These mysteries are exalted in wisdom, and the soul enters the knowledge of them, engulfing and immersing herself in them. And both the bride and bridegroom will taste the savor and the delight caused by the knowledge of these mysteries together with the powers and attributes of God uncovered in them such as justice, mercy, wisdom, power, charity, and so on.

> And then we will go on
> To the high caverns in the rock

The rock mentioned here, as St. Paul says, is Christ [1 Cor. 10:4]. The high caverns of this rock are the sublime, exalted, and deep mysteries of God's wisdom in Christ, in the hypostatic union of the human nature with the divine Word, and in the corresponding union of human beings with God, and the mystery of the harmony between God's justice and mercy with respect to the manifestations of his judgments in the salvation of the human race. These mysteries are so profound that she very appropriately calls them high caverns; high, because of the height of the sublime mysteries; caverns, because of the depth of God's wisdom in them. As caverns are deep and have many recesses, so each of the mysteries in Christ is singularly deep in wisdom and contains many recesses of his secret judgments of predestination and foreknowledge concerning the children of this earth. She then adds:

Which are so well concealed. They are so well concealed that however numerous are the mysteries and marvels that holy doctors have discovered and saintly souls understood in this earthly life, all the more is yet to be said and understood. There is much to fathom in Christ, for he is like an abundant mine with many recesses of treasures, so that however deep people go they never reach the end or bottom, but rather in every recess find new veins with new riches everywhere. On this account St. Paul said of Christ: "In Christ dwell hidden all treasures and wisdom" [Col. 2:3]. The soul cannot enter these caverns or reach these treasures if, as we said, she does not first pass over to the divine wisdom through the straits of exterior and interior suffering. For one cannot reach in this life what is attainable of these mysteries of Christ without having suffered much, and without having received numerous intellectual and sensible favors from God, and without having undergone much spiritual activity; for all these favors are inferior to the wisdom of the mysteries of Christ in that they serve as preparations for coming to this wisdom. When Moses asked God to reveal his glory, he was told by God that he would be unable to receive such a revelation in this life, but that he would be shown all good, that is, all the good revealable in this life. So God put Moses in the cavern of the rock, which is Christ, as we said, and showed his back to him, which was to impart knowledge of the mysteries of the humanity of Christ.

The soul, then, earnestly longs to enter these caverns of Christ in order to be absorbed, transformed, and wholly inebriated in the love of the wisdom of these mysteries and hide herself in the bosom of the beloved. In the Song of Songs he invites her to these clefts, saying: "Arise, make haste, my love, my beautiful one, and come into the clefts of the rock and into the cavern of the wall" [Song of Sol. 2:13–14]. . . .

Stanza 38

Introduction

In the two preceding stanzas the bride's song focused on the good that the bridegroom will offer her in that eternal bliss; that is, the spouse will really transform her into the beauty of both his created and uncreated wisdom, and also into the beauty of the union of the Word with his humanity, in which she will know him face to face as well as from the back.

In the next stanza she discusses two things: first, the manner in which she will taste that divine juice of the sapphires, or rather the pomegranates; second, the glory she will give to her bridegroom through her predestination.

It should be noted that even though she refers to these goods as successive parts, they are all contained in one essential glory. She says:

> There you will show me
> What my soul has been seeking,
> And then you will give me,
> You, my life, will give me there
> What you gave me on that other day.

Commentary

The reason the soul desired to enter these caverns was to reach the consummation of the love of God, which she had always been seeking; that is, to love God as purely and perfectly as he loves her in order to repay him by such love. She declares to the bridegroom in this stanza that there he will show her what was her desire in all her acts, how to love the spouse as perfectly as he loves her. The second gift she will receive there is the essential glory to which he predestined her from the day of his eternity.

Thus she declares:

> There you will show me
> What my soul has been seeking

The soul's aim is a love equal to God's. She always desired this equality, naturally and supernaturally, for lovers cannot be satisfied if they fail to feel that they love as much as they are loved. Since the soul sees that through her transformation in God in this life she cannot, even though her love is immense, equal the perfection of God's love for her, she desires the clear transformation of glory in which she will reach this equality. Even though there is a true union of will in this high state she now enjoys, she cannot attain the excellence and power of love that she will possess in the strong union of glory. Just as the soul, according to St. Paul, will know then as she is known by God [1 Cor. 13:12], so she will also love God as she is loved by him. As her intellect will be the intellect of God, her will then will be God's will, and thus her love will be God's love. The soul's will is not destroyed there, but it is so firmly united with the strength of God's will, with which he loves her, that her love for him is as strong and perfect as his love for her, for the two wills are so united that there is only one will and love, which is God's. This strength lies in the Holy Spirit, in whom the soul is there transformed, for by this transformation of glory he supplies what is lacking in her, since he is given to the soul for the sake of the strength of this love. Even in the perfect transformation of this state of spiritual marriage, which the soul reaches in this life, she superabounds with grace and, as above, loves in some way through the Holy Spirit who is given [Rom. 5:5] in this transformation of love.

It should be noted that the soul does not say that there he will give her his love—although he really does—because she would in this way manifest only that God loves her. She states, rather, that there he will show her how to love him as perfectly as she desires. Insofar as he gives her there his love, he shows her how to love as she is loved by him. God makes her love him with the very strength with which he loves her. Transforming her into his love, as we said, he gives her his own strength by which she can love him. As if he were to put an instrument in her hands and show her how it works by operating it jointly with her, he shows her how to love and gives her the ability to do so. . . .

Stanza 39

The breathing of the air,
The song of the sweet nightingale,
The grove and its living beauty
In the serene night,
With a flame that is consuming and painless. . . .

Commentary

The breathing of the air. This breathing of the air is an ability that the soul states God will give her there in the communication of the Holy Spirit. By his divine breathlike spiration, the Holy Spirit elevates the soul sublimely and informs her and makes her capable of breathing in God the same spiration of love that the Father breathes in the Son and the Son in the Father, which is the Holy Spirit himself, who in the Father and the Son breathes out to her in this transformation, in order to unite her to himself. There would not be a true and total transformation if the soul were not transformed in the three Persons of the Most Holy Trinity in an open and manifest degree.

And this kind of spiration of the Holy Spirit in the soul, by which God transforms her into himself, is so sublime, delicate, and deep a delight that a mortal tongue finds it indescribable, nor can the human intellect, as such, in any way grasp it. Even that which comes to pass in the communication given in this temporal transformation is unspeakable, for the soul united and transformed in God breathes out in God to God the very divine spiration that God—she being transformed in him—breathes out in himself to her.

In the transformation that the soul possesses in this life, the same spiration passes from God to the soul and from the soul to God with notable frequency and blissful love, although not in the open and manifest degree proper to the next life. Such I believe was St. Paul's meaning when he said: "Since you are children of God, God sent the Spirit of his Son into your hearts, calling to the Father" [Gal. 4:6]. This is true of the Blessed in the next life and of the perfect in this life according to the ways described.

One should not think it impossible that the soul be capable of so sublime an activity as this breathing in God, through participation, as God breathes in her. For, granted that God favors her by union with the Most Blessed Trinity, in which she becomes deiform and God through participation, how could it be incredible that she also understand, know, and love—or, better, that this be done in her—in the Trinity, together with it, as does the Trinity itself! Yet God accomplishes this in the soul through communication and participation. This is transformation in the three Persons in power and wisdom and love, and thus the soul is like God through this transformation. He created her in his image and likeness that she might attain such resemblance. . . .

In the serene night. This night is the contemplation in which the soul desires to behold these things. Because of its obscurity, she calls contemplation night. On this account contemplation is also termed mystical theology, meaning the secret or hidden knowledge of God. In contemplation God teaches the soul very quietly and secretly, without its knowing how, without the sound of words, and without the help of any bodily or spiritual faculty, in silence and quietude, in darkness to all sensory and natural things. Some spiritual persons call this contemplation knowing by unknowing. For this knowledge is not produced by the intellect that the philosophers call the agent intellect, which works on the forms, fantasies, and apprehensions of the corporal faculties; rather, it is produced in the possible or passive intellect. This possible intellect, without the reception of these forms and so on, receives passively only substantial knowledge, which is divested of images and given without any work or active function of the intellect.

This contemplation, in which the soul, by means of her transformation, has sublime knowledge in this life of the divine grove and its living beauty, is consequently called night. Yet, however sublime this knowledge may be, it is still a dark night when compared with the beatific knowledge she asks for here. In seeking clear contemplation, she asks that this enjoyment of the grove and its fascination, as well as the other goods mentioned, take place now in the serene night, that is, in beatific and clear contemplation, the night of the dark contemplation of this earth changing into the contemplation of the clear and serene vision of God in heaven. Therefore, by saying "in the serene night," she means in the clear and serene contemplation of the vision of God. David declares of this night of contemplation: "The night will be my illumination in my delights" [Ps. 139:11-12], which is like saying: "When I shall delight in the essential vision of God, then the night of contemplation will have changed into day and light for my intellect."

With a flame that is consuming and painless. By the flame she here indicates the love of the Holy Spirit. To consummate means to bring to completion or perfection. The soul, then, in affirming that the beloved will give her all the things she mentioned in this stanza, and that she will possess them with consummate and perfect love, and that these goods will all be absorbed—and she with them—in perfect love that is painless, affirms all this in order to reveal the complete perfection of this love. For love to be perfect it must have these two properties: it must consummate and transform the soul in God; and the inflaming and transformation engendered by this flame must give no pain to the soul, which cannot be true except in the beatific state where this flame is delightful love. For by the transformation of the soul in this flame, there is a beatific conformity and satisfaction of both lover and beloved, and thus the flame gives no pain from the variety of greater or less intensity, as it did before the soul reached the capacity of this perfect love. Having reached perfection, the soul possesses a love so comforting and conformed to God that, even though God is a consuming fire, as Moses says [Deut. 4:24], he is now a consummator and restorer. This transformation is not like the one the soul possesses in this life, for although the flame in this life is very perfect and consummating in love, it is still also somewhat consuming and destructive, acting as fire does on coal; although the coal is conformed with and transformed into the fire, and does not fume as it did before the transformation, still the flame which consummated the coal in fire consumed and reduced it to ashes.

Stanza 40

No one looked at her,
Nor did Aminadab appear;
The siege was still;
And the cavalry,
At the sight of the waters, descended.

Introduction and Commentary

The bride knows that now her will's desire is detached from all things and attached to her God in most intimate love; that the sensory part of her soul, with all its strength, faculties, and appetites, is in harmony with the spirit, and its rebelliousness brought into subjection; that the devil is now conquered and far withdrawn as a result of her varied and prolonged spiritual activity and combat; that her soul is united and transformed with an abundance of heavenly riches and gifts; and that consequently she is now well prepared, disposed, and strong, leaning on her beloved, coming up from the desert of death, flowing with delights, to the glorious thrones of her bridegroom [Song of Sol. 8:5]. Desiring the spouse to conclude this matter now, she sets all these facts before him in this last stanza in order to urge him the more to do so. In this stanza she mentions five blessings:

First, her soul is detached and withdrawn from all things.

Second, the devil is conquered and put to flight.

Third, the passions are subjected and the natural appetites mortified.

Fourth and fifth, the sensory and lower part is reformed, puri-fied, and brought into conformity with the spiritual part. The sensory part not only offers no obstacle to the reception of these spiritual blessings, but is even accommodated to them, since it participates according to its capacity in the goods the soul now possesses. . . .

The bride sets all this perfection and preparedness before her beloved, the Son of God, with the desire that he transfer her from the spiritual marriage, to which he desired to bring her in this Church Militant [the church on earth], to the glorious marriage of the Triumphant [the church in heaven]. May the most sweet Jesus, bridegroom of faithful souls, be pleased to bring all who invoke his name to this glorious marriage. To him be honor and glory, together with the Father and the Holy Spirit, in *saecula saeculorum* [forever and ever]. Amen.

THE LIVING FLAME
OF LOVE

A commentary on the stanzas that treat the
very intimate and exalted union and transformation of the soul in God, written at the
request of Doña Ana de Peñalosa by the
author of the stanzas.

Prologue

I have felt, very noble and devout lady, somewhat reluctant to explain these four stanzas, as you asked. Since they deal with matters so interior and spiritual, for which words are usually lacking—in that the spiritual surpasses sense—I find it difficult to say something of their content. Also one speaks badly of the intimate depths of the spirit if one does not do so with a deeply recollected soul. Because of my want of such recollection, I have deferred this commentary until now, a period in which the Lord seems to have uncovered some knowledge and bestowed some fervor. This must be the result of your holy desires; perhaps since I have composed the stanzas for you, His Majesty wants me to explain them for you.

I have been encouraged in knowing certainly that through my own ability I shall say nothing worthwhile, especially in matters so sublime and vital, and thus only the faults and mistakes of this commentary will be mine. Submitting it to the judgment and better opinion of our Holy Mother the Roman Catholic Church, by whose rule no one errs, depending on sacred Scripture, and knowing the reader understands that everything I say is as far from the reality as is a painting from the living object represented, I will venture to declare what I know.

There is no reason to marvel at God's granting such sublime and strange gifts to souls he determines to favor. If we consider that he is God and that he bestows them as God, with infinite love and goodness, it does not seem unreasonable. For he declared that the

Father, the Son, and the Holy Spirit would take up their abode in anyone who loved him [John 14:23]. He takes up his abode in individuals by making them live the life of God and dwell in the Father, the Son, and the Holy Spirit, as the soul points out in these stanzas.

Although in the stanzas we have already commented on, we speak of the highest degree of perfection one can reach in this life (transformation in God), these stanzas treat a love within this very state of transformation that is more exalted and perfect. Even though it is true that what these and other stanzas describe is all one state of transformation, and that as such one cannot pass beyond it; yet, with time and practice, love can receive added quality, as I say, and become more intensified. We have an example of this in the activity of fire: although the fire has penetrated the wood, transformed it, and united it with itself, yet as this fire grows hotter and continues to burn, the wood becomes much more incandescent and inflamed, even to the point of flaring up and shooting out flames from itself.

It should be understood that the soul now speaking has reached this enkindled degree, and is so inwardly transformed and exalted in the fire of love that it is not merely united to this fire, but produces within it a living flame. The soul feels this and speaks of it thus in these stanzas with intimate and delicate sweetness of love, burning in love's flame, and stressing in these stanzas some of its effects.

I will use in this commentary the method I have used before. First I will quote all the stanzas together, and then, after recording each stanza separately, I will present a brief explanation of it; finally, I will quote each verse and comment on it.

Stanzas That the Soul Recites in the Intimate Union with God

1. O living flame of love
That tenderly wounds my soul
In its deepest center! Since
Now you are not oppressive,
Now Consummate! if it be your will:
Tear through the veil of this sweet encounter!

2. O sweet cautery,
O delightful wound!
O gentle hand! O delicate touch
That tastes of eternal life
And pays every debt!
In killing you changed death to life.

3. O lamps of fire!
In whose splendors
The deep caverns of feeling,
Once obscure and blind,
Now give forth, so rarely, so exquisitely,
Both warmth and light to their beloved.

4. How gently and lovingly
You wake in my heart,
Where in secret you dwell alone;
And in your sweet breathing,
Filled with good and glory,
How tenderly you swell my heart with love!

Stanza 1

O living flame of love
That tenderly wounds my soul
In its deepest center! Since
Now you are not oppressive,
Now Consummate! if it be your will:
Tear through the veil of this sweet encounter!

Commentary

The soul now feels that it is all inflamed in the divine union and that its palate is all bathed in glory and love, that in the most intimate part of its substance it is flooded with no less than rivers of glory, abounding in delights, and that from its bosom flow rivers of living water [John 7:38], which the Son of God declared will rise up in such souls. Accordingly it seems, because the soul is so vigorously transformed in God, so sublimely possessed by him and arrayed with such rich gifts and virtues, that it is singularly close to beatitude—so close that only a thin veil separates it.

And the soul sees that every time that delicate flame of love, burning within, assails it, it does so as though glorifying it with gentle and powerful glory. Such is the glory this flame of love imparts that each time it absorbs and attacks, it seems that it is about to give eternal life and tear the veil of mortal life, that very little is lacking, and that because of this lack the soul does not receive eternal glory completely. Hence with ardent desire the soul tells the flame, the Holy Spirit, to tear now the veil of mortal life by that sweet encounter in which he truly communicates entirely what he is seemingly about to give each time he encounters it, that is, complete and perfect glory. And thus it says:

O living flame of love. To lay stress on the sentiment and esteem with which it speaks in these four stanzas, the soul uses in all of them the exclamations "O" and "how," which stress affection. Each time they are uttered, they reveal more about the interior than the tongue expresses. "O" serves to speak of intense desire and to use persuasion in petitioning. The soul uses this expression for both reasons in this stanza, because it intimates and stresses its immense desire, persuading love to loose it.

This flame of love is the Spirit of its bridegroom, which is the Holy Spirit. The soul feels him within itself not only as a fire which has consumed and transformed it, but as a fire that burns and flares within it, as I mentioned. And that flame, every time it flares up, bathes the soul in glory and refreshes it with the quality of divine life. Such is the activity of the Holy Spirit in the soul transformed in love: the interior acts he produces shoot up flames, for they are acts of inflamed love in which the will of the soul united with that flame, made one with it, loves most sublimely.

Thus these acts of love are most precious; one of them is more meritorious and valuable than all the deeds one may have performed in the whole of life before this transformation, however great they may have been.

The same difference that lies between a habit and an act lies between the transformation in love and the flame of love; it is like the difference between the wood that is on fire and the flame that leaps up from it, for the flame is the effect of the fire that is present there.

Hence we can compare the soul in its ordinary condition in this state of transformation of love to the log of wood that is ever immersed in fire, and the acts of this soul to the flame that blazes up from the fire of love. The more intense the fire of union, the more vehemently does this fire burst into flames. The acts of the will are united to this flame and ascend, carried away and absorbed in the flame of the Holy Spirit, just as the angel mounted to God in the flame of Manoah's sacrifice [Judg. 13:20].

Thus in this state the soul cannot make acts because the Holy Spirit makes them all and moves it toward them. As a result all the acts of the soul are divine, since the movement toward these acts and their execution stem from God. Hence the soul thinks that every time this flame shoots up, making it love with delight and divine quality, that it is being given eternal life, since it is being raised by the flame to the activity of God in God.

This is the language and these the words God speaks in souls that are purged, cleansed, and all enkindled. As David exclaimed: "Your word is exceedingly enkindled" [Ps. 119:139], and the prophet: "Are not my words, perchance, like a fire?" [Jer. 23:29]. As God himself says through St. John, these words are spirit and life [John 6:63]. This spirit and life is perceived by souls who have ears to hear it, those souls, as I say, that are cleansed and enamored. Those who do not have a sound palate, but seek other tastes, cannot taste the spirit and life of God's words; His words, rather, are distasteful to them.

Hence the loftier were the words of the Son of God, the more tasteless they were to the impure, as happened when he preached the savory and loving doctrine of the Holy Eucharist; for many turned away [John 6:60–61, 66].

Those who do not taste this language God speaks within them must not think on this account that others do not taste it. St. Peter tasted it in his soul when he said to Christ: "Lord, where shall we go; you have the words of eternal life?" [John 6:68]. And the Samaritan woman forgot the water and the water pot because of the sweetness of God's words [John 4:28].

Since this soul is so close to God that it is transformed into a flame of love, in which the Father, the Son, and the Holy Spirit are communicated to it, what is so unbelievable about saying that it enjoys a foretaste of eternal life? Yet it does not enjoy this perfectly, since the conditions of life here below do not allow for this. But the delight that the flaring up of the Holy Spirit generates in the soul is so sublime that it makes the soul know that which savors of eternal life. Thus it refers to this flame as living, not because the flame is not always living, but because of this effect; it makes the soul live in God spiritually and experience the life of God in the manner David mentions: "My heart and my flesh rejoiced in the living God" [Ps. 84:2]. David did not refer to God as living because of a necessity to do so, for God is always living, but in order to manifest that the spirit and the senses, transformed in God, enjoy him in a living way, which is to taste the living God—that is God's life, eternal life. Nor did David call him the living God other than because he enjoyed him in a living way, although not perfectly, but as though by a glimpse of eternal life. Thus in this flame the soul experiences God so vividly and tastes him with such delight and sweetness that it exclaims: "O living flame of love!"

That tenderly wounds my soul. That is: "O living flame of love that with your ardor tenderly touches me." Since this flame is a flame of divine life, it wounds the soul with the tenderness of God's life, and it wounds and stirs it so deeply as to make it dissolve in love. What the bride affirmed in the Song of Songs is fulfilled in the soul. She was so moved that her soul melted, and thus she says: "As soon as he spoke my soul melted" [Song of Sol. 5:4]. For God's speech is the effect he produces in the soul.

But how can one claim that the flame wounds the soul, since there is nothing left in it to wound now that it is all cauterized with the fire of love? It is something splendid that, since love is never idle, but in continual motion, it is always emitting flames everywhere like a blazing fire, and, since its duty is to wound in order to cause love and delight, and it is present in this soul as a living flame, it dispatches its wounds like most tender flares of delicate love. Joyfully and festively it practices the arts and games of love, as though in the palace of its nuptials, as Ahasuerus did with Esther [Esther 2:17–18]. God shows his graces there, manifests his riches and the glory of his grandeur that in this soul might be fulfilled what he asserted in Proverbs: "I was delighted every day, playing before him all the time, playing in the world. And my delights were to be with the children of men" [Prov. 8:30–31], that is, by bestowing delights on them. Hence these wounds (his games) are flames of tender touches; arising from the fire of love, which is not idle, they suddenly touch the soul. These, it says, occur inwardly and wound the soul.

In its *deepest center!* This feast takes place in the substance of the soul, where neither the center of the senses nor the devil can reach. Therefore, it is the more secure, substantial, and delightful, the more interior it is, because the more interior it is, the purer it is. And the greater the purity, the more abundantly, frequently, and generously God communicates himself. Thus the delight and joy of the soul is so much the more intense because God is the doer of all without the soul's doing anything. Since the soul cannot do any work of its own save by the means and aid of the corporal senses, from which in this event it is very free and far removed, its sole occupation now is to receive from God, who alone can move the soul and do his work in its depths. Thus all the movements of this soul are divine. Although they belong to it, they belong to it because God works them in it and with it, for it wills and consents to them. . . .

It is noteworthy, then, that love is the soul's inclination, strength, and power in making its way to God, for love unites it with God. The more degrees of love it has, the more deeply it enters into God and centers itself in him. We can say that there are as many centers in God possible to the soul, each one deeper than the other, as there are degrees of love of God possible to it. A stronger love is a more unitive love, and we can understand in this manner the many dwelling places the Son of God declared were in his Father's house [John 14:2].

Hence, that the soul be in its center—which is God, as we have said—it is sufficient for it to possess one degree of love, for by one degree alone it is united with him through grace. Should it have two degrees, it will have become united and concentrated in God in another deeper center. Should it reach three, it will have centered itself in a third. But once it has attained the final degree, God's love will have arrived at wounding the soul in its ultimate and deepest center, which is to transform and clarify it in its whole being, power, and strength, and according to its capacity, until it appears to be God.

When light shines on a clean and pure crystal, we find that the more intense the degree of light, the more light the crystal has concentrated within it and the brighter it becomes; it can become so brilliant due to the abundance of light it receives that it seems to be all light. And then the crystal is indistinguishable from the light, since it is illumined according to its full capacity, which is to appear to be light. . . .

And it should not be held as incredible in a soul now examined, purged, and tried in the fire of tribulations, trials, and many kinds of temptations, and found faithful in love, that the promise of the Son of God be fulfilled, the promise that the Most Blessed Trinity will come and dwell within anyone who loves him [John 14:23]. The Blessed Trinity inhabits the soul by divinely illumining its intellect with the wisdom of the Son, delighting its will in the Holy Spirit, and by absorbing it powerfully and mightily in the delightful embrace of the Father's sweetness.

If he acts thus in some souls, as it is true he does, it should be believed that this soul we are speaking of will not be left behind in regard to receiving these favors from God. For what we are explaining about the activity of the Holy Spirit within it is something far greater than what occurs in the communication and transformation of love. This latter resembles the glowing embers, whereas the former is similar to embers not merely glowing, but embers that have become so hot they shoot forth a living flame.

And thus these two kinds of union (union of love alone, and union with an inflaming of love) are somehow comparable to the fire of God that, Isaiah says, is on Zion and to his furnace that is in Jerusalem [Isa. 31:9]. The one signifies the Church Militant, in which the fire of charity is not enkindled to an extreme; the other signifies the vision of peace, which is the Church Triumphant, where this fire is like a furnace blazing in the perfection of love.

Although, as we said, the soul has not attained such great perfection as this vision of peace, yet, in comparison with the other common union, this union resembles a blazing furnace in which there is a vision so much more peaceful and glorious and tender, just as the flame is clearer and more resplendent than the burning coal.

Wherefore the soul, feeling that this living flame of love is vividly communicating to it every good, since this divine love carries all things with it, exclaims: "O living flame of love that tenderly wounds my soul." This is like saying: "O enkindled love, with your loving movements you are pleasantly glorifying me according to the greater capacity and strength of my soul, bestowing divine knowledge according to all the ability and capacity of my intellect, and communicating love according to the greater power of my will, and rejoicing the substance of my soul with the torrent of your delight by your divine contact and substantial union, in harmony with the greater purity of my substance and the capacity and breadth of my memory!"

And this is what happens, in an indescribable way, at the time this flame of love rises up within the soul. Since the soul is completely purged in its substance and faculties (memory, intellect, and will), the divine substance, which because of its purity, as the Wise Man says, touches everywhere profoundly, subtly, and sublimely [Wis. 7:24], absorbs the soul in itself with its divine flame. And in that immersion of the soul in wisdom, the Holy Spirit sets in motion the glorious flickerings of his flame. . . .

However intimate the union with God may be, individuals will never have satisfaction and rest until God's glory appears [Ps. 17:15], especially since they now experience its savor and sweetness. This experience is so intense that if God had not favored their flesh by fortifying the sensory part with His right hand, as He did Moses in the rock, enabling him to behold His glory without dying [Exod. 33:22], nature would be torn apart and death would ensue, since the lower part is unequipped to suffer so much and such a sublime fire of glory.

> Since now you are not oppressive,
> Now Consummate! if it be your will.

Affliction, then, does not accompany this desire and petition, for the soul is no longer capable of such affliction, but with a gentle and delightful desire it seeks this in the conformity of both spirit and sense to God's will. As a result it says in this verse,

"Now Consummate! if it be your will," for its will and appetite are so united with God that it considers the fulfillment of God's will to be its glory.

Yet the sudden flashes of glory and love that appear vaguely in these touches at the door of entry into the soul, and which are unable to fit into it because of the narrowness of the earthly house, are so sublime that it would rather be a sign of little love not to try to enter into that perfection and completion of love.

Moreover, a soul is conscious that in that vigor of the bridegroom's delightful communication, the Holy Spirit rouses and invites it by the immense glory he marvelously and with gentle affection places before its eyes, telling it what he told the bride in the Song of Songs. The bride thus refers to this: "Behold what my spouse is saying to me: 'Arise and make haste, my love, my dove, my beautiful one, and come'" [Song of Sol. 2:10]. . . .

Tear through the veil of this sweet encounter! The veil is what impedes so singular an event. It is easy to reach God when all the impediments are removed and the veils that separate the soul from union with him are torn. We can say there are three veils that constitute a hindrance to this union with God, and which must be torn if the union is to be effected and possessed perfectly by the soul, that is: the temporal veil, comprising all creatures; the natural, embodying the purely natural inclinations and operations; and the sensitive, which consists only of the union of the soul with the body, that is, the sensitive and animal life of which St. Paul speaks: "We know that if this our earthly house is dissolved, we have a building of God in heaven" [2 Cor. 5:1].

The first two veils must necessarily be torn in order to obtain this union with God in which all the things of the world are renounced, all the natural appetites and affections mortified, and the natural operations of the soul divinized.

All of this was accomplished, and these veils were torn by means of the oppressive encounters of this flame. Through the spiritual purgation we referred to above, the soul tears these two veils completely and is united with God, as it here is; only the third veil of this sensitive life remains to be torn. As a result it mentions a veil and not veils, since there is only this one to tear. Because the veil is now so tenuous, thin, and spiritualized through this union with God, the flame is not harsh in its encounter, as it was with the other two, but savorous and sweet. The soul, hence, calls it a sweet encounter; so much the sweeter and more savorous, the more it seems about to tear through the veil of mortal life.

It should be known that the death of persons who have reached this state is far different in its cause and mode than the death of others, even though it is similar in natural circumstances. If the death of other people is caused by sickness or old age, the death of these persons is not so induced, in spite of their being sick or old; their soul is not wrested from them unless by some impetus and encounter of love, far more sublime than previous ones, of greater power, and more valiant, since it tears through this veil and carries off the jewel, which is the soul.

The death of such persons is very gentle and very sweet, sweeter and more gentle than was their whole spiritual life on earth. For they die with the most sublime impulses and delightful encounters of love, resembling the swan whose song is much sweeter at the moment of death. Accordingly, David affirmed that the death of the saints is precious in the sight of the Lord [Ps. 116:15]. The soul's riches gather together here, and its rivers of love move on to enter the sea, for these rivers, because they are blocked, become so vast that they themselves resemble seas. The first treasures of the just and their last are heaped together to accompany them when they depart and go off to their kingdom, while praises are heard from the ends of the earth, which, as Isaiah says, are the glory of the just one [Isa. 24:16].

The soul, then, conscious of the abundance of its enrichment, feels at the time of these glorious encounters to be almost at the point of departing for the complete and perfect possession of its kingdom, for it knows that it is pure, rich, full of virtues, and prepared for such a kingdom. God permits it in this state to discern its beauty, and he entrusts to it the gifts and virtues he has bestowed, for everything is converted into love and praises. And the soul has no touch of presumption or vanity, since it no longer bears the leaven of imperfection, which corrupts the mass [1 Cor. 5:6; Gal. 5:9]. Since it is aware that nothing is wanting other than to tear the weak veil of this natural life, in which it feels the entanglement, hindrance, and captivity of its freedom, and since it desires to be dissolved and to be with Christ [Phil 1:23], it laments that a life so weak and base impedes another so mighty and sublime and asks that the veil be torn, saying: "Tear through the veil of this sweet encounter!"

There are three reasons for the term "veil": first, because of the union between the spirit and the flesh; second, because this union separates the soul from God; third, because a veil is not so thick and opaque that a brilliant light cannot shine through it; and in this state the bond seems to be so tenuous a veil, since it is now very spiritual, thin, and luminous, that it does not prevent the divinity from vaguely appearing through it. Since the soul perceives the power of the other life, it is conscious of the weakness of this one and that the veil is of delicate fabric, as thin as a spider's web; in David's words: "Our years shall be considered as the spider" [Ps. 90:9], and according to Isaiah, all nations are as though they were not [Isa. 40:17]. These things carry the same weight in the soul's view: all things are nothing to it, and it is nothing in its own eyes; God alone is its all. . . .

Stanza 2

> O sweet cautery,
> O delightful wound!
> O gentle hand! O delicate touch
> That tastes of eternal life
> And pays every debt!
> In killing you changed death to life.

Commentary

In this stanza the soul proclaims how the three Persons of the Most Blessed Trinity, the Father, the Son, and the Holy Spirit, are they who effect in it this divine work of union. Thus the hand, the cautery, and the touch are substantially the same. The soul applies these terms to the Persons of the Trinity because of the effect each of the Persons produces. The cautery is the Holy Spirit; the hand is the Father; and the touch is the Son. The soul here magnifies the Father, the Son, and the Holy Spirit, stressing the three admirable favors and blessings they produce in it, having changed its death to life, transforming it in the Trinity. . . .

> O sweet cautery,
> O delightful wound!

O happy wound, wrought by One who knows only how to heal! O fortunate and choicest wound; you were made only for delight, and the quality of your affliction is delight and gratification for the wounded soul! You are great, O delightful wound, because he who caused you is great! And your delight is great because the fire of love is infinite and makes you delightful according to your capacity and greatness. O, then, delightful wound, so much more sublimely delightful the more the cautery touched the intimate center of the substance of the soul, burning all that was burnable in order to give delight to all that could be delighted!

It is understandable that this cautery and this wound are of the highest degree possible in this state. For there are many other ways God cauterizes the soul that are unlike this one and fail to reach such a degree. For this cautery is a touch only of the divinity in the soul, without any intellectual or imaginative form or figure.

There is another way of cauterizing the soul by an intellectual form, usually very sublime, which is as follows. It will happen that while the soul is inflamed with the love of God, although not with a love of as deep a quality as that we mentioned (yet it is fitting that it be so for what I want to say), it will feel that a seraph is assailing it by means of an arrow or dart that is all afire with love. And the seraph pierces and cauterizes this soul which, like a red-hot coal, or, better, a flame, is already enkindled. And then in this cauterization, when the soul is transpierced with that dart, the flame gushes forth, vehemently and with a sudden ascent, like the fire in a furnace or an oven when someone uses a poker or bellows to stir and excite it. And being wounded by this fiery dart, the soul feels the wound with unsurpassable delight. Besides being fully stirred in great sweetness by the blowing or impetuous motion of the seraph, in which it feels in its intense ardor to be dissolving in love, it is aware of the delicate wound and the herb (which serves as a keen temper to the dart) as though it were a sharp point in the substance of the spirit, in the heart of the pierced soul.

Who can fittingly speak of this intimate point of the wound, which seems to be in the middle of the heart of the spirit, there where the soul experiences the excellence of the delight? The soul feels that that point is like a tiny mustard seed, very much alive and enkindled, sending into its surroundings a living and enkindled fire of love. The fire issuing from the substance and power of that living point, which contains the substance and power of the herb, is felt to be subtly diffused through all the spiritual and substantial veins of the soul in the measure of the soul's power and strength. The soul feels its ardor strengthen and increase and its love become so refined in this ardor that seemingly there are seas of loving fire within it, reaching to the heights and depths of the earthly and heavenly spheres, imbuing all with love. It seems to it that the entire universe is a sea of love in which it is engulfed, for, conscious of the living point or center of love within itself, it is unable to catch sight of the boundaries of this love.

There is nothing else to say about the soul's enjoyment here except that it realizes how appropriately the kingdom of heaven was compared in the gospel to a grain of mustard seed which, by reason of its intense heat, grows into a large tree, despite its being so small [Matt. 13:31–32]. For the soul is converted into an immense fire of love, which emanates from that enkindled point at the heart of the spirit.

Few persons have reached these heights. Some have, however; especially those whose virtue and spirit were to be diffused among their children. For God accords to founders, with respect to the first fruits of the spirit, wealth and value commensurate with the greater or lesser following they will have in their doctrine and spirituality.

Let us return to the work of that seraph, for he truly inflicts a sore and wounds inwardly in the spirit. Thus, if God sometimes permits an effect to extend to the bodily senses in the fashion in which it existed interiorly, the wound and sore appear outwardly, as happened when the seraph wounded St. Francis. When the soul is wounded with love by the five wounds, the effect extends to the body and these wounds are impressed on the body, and it is wounded just as the soul is wounded with love. God usually does not bestow a favor on the body without bestowing it first and principally on the soul. Thus the greater the delight and strength of love the wound produces in the soul, so much the greater is that produced by the wound outside on the body, and when there is an increase in one, there is an increase in the other. This so happens because these souls are purified and established in God, and that which is a cause of pain and torment to their corruptible flesh is sweet and delectable to their strong and healthy spirit. It is, then, a wonderful experience to feel the pain augment with the delight.

Job, with his wounds, clearly beheld this marvel when he said to God: "Returning to me, you torment me wondrously" [Job 10:16]. This is an unspeakable marvel and worthy of the abundance and sweetness God has hidden for them that fear him [Ps. 31:19]: to cause them to enjoy so much the more savor and sweetness, the more pain and torment they experience.

Nevertheless, when the wound is made only in the soul without being communicated outwardly, the delight can be more intense and sublime. The spirit has the flesh curbed in this state, but when the goods of the spirit are communicated also to the flesh, the flesh pulls the reins, bridles the mouth of this swift horse of the spirit, and restrains its great impetuosity; for if the spirit makes use of its power, the reins will break. Yet until the reins are broken, the flesh does not fail to oppress the spirit's freedom, as the Wise Man asserts: "The corruptible body is a load on the soul, and the earthly dwelling oppresses the spiritual mind which of itself comprehends many things" [Wis. 9:15].

I say this in order to make it clear that he who would go to God relying on natural ability and reasoning will not be very spiritual.

There are some who think that by pure force and the activity of the senses, which of themselves are lowly and no more than natural, they can reach the strength and height of the supernatural spirit. One does not attain to this peak without restraining and leaving aside the activity of the senses.

Yet it is something quite different when an effect of the spirit overflows in the senses. When this is true, the effect in the senses proceeds from an abundance of spirit, as in the event of the wounds that proceed from the inner strength and appear outwardly. This happened with St. Paul, whose immense compassion for the sufferings of Christ redounded into the body, as he explains to the Galatians: "I bear the wounds of the Lord Jesus in my body" [Gal. 6:17]. . . .

O gentle hand! O delicate touch. And your only begotten Son, O merciful hand of the Father, is the delicate touch by which you touched me with the force of your cautery and wounded me.

O you, then, delicate touch, the Word, the Son of God, through the delicacy of your divine being, you subtly penetrate the substance of my soul and, lightly touching it all, absorb it entirely in yourself in divine modes of delights and sweetnesses unheard of in the land of Canaan and never before seen in Teman [Bar. 3:22]! O, then, very delicate, exceedingly delicate, touch of the Word, so much the more delicate for me insofar as, after overthrowing the mountains and smashing the rocks to pieces on Mount Horeb with the shadow of might and power that went before you, you gave the prophet the sweetest and strongest experience of yourself in the gentle breeze [1 Kings 19:11–12]! O gentle breeze, since you are a delicate and mild breeze, tell us: How do you, the Word, the Son of God, touch mildly and gently, since you are so awesome and mighty? Oh, happy is the soul that you, being terrible and strong, gently and lightly touch! Proclaim this to the world! But you are unwilling to proclaim this to the world because it does not know of a mild breeze and will not experience you, for it can neither receive nor see you [John 14:17]. But they, O my God and my life, will see and experience your mild touch, who withdraw from the world and become mild, bringing the mild into harmony with the mild, thus enabling themselves to experience and enjoy you. You touch them the more gently, the more you dwell permanently hidden within them, for the substance of their soul is now refined, cleansed, and purified, withdrawn from every creature and every touch and trace of creature. As a result, "You hide them in the secret of your face," which is the Word, "from the disturbance of men" [Ps. 31:20].

O, then again, repeatedly delicate touch, so much the stronger and mightier, the more you are delicate! Since you detach and withdraw the soul from all the other touches of created things by the might of your delicacy, and both reserve it for and unite it to yourself alone, you leave so mild an effect in the soul that every other touch of all things both high and low seems coarse and spurious. It displeases the soul to look at these things, and to deal with them is a heavy pain and torment to it. . . .

That tastes of eternal life. Although that which the soul tastes in this touch of God is not perfect, it does in fact have a certain savor of eternal life, as was mentioned. And this is not incredible if we believe, as we should, that this is a touch of substances, that is, of the substance of God in the substance of the soul. Many saints have attained to this substantial touch during their lives on earth. . . .

And pays every debt! The soul affirms this because in the taste of eternal life, which it here enjoys, it feels the reward for the trials it passed through in order to reach this state. It feels not only that it has been compensated and satisfied justly, but that it has been rewarded exceedingly. It thoroughly understands the truth of the bridegroom's promise in the gospel, that he would repay a hundredfold [Matt. 19:29]. It has endured no tribulation, or penance, or trial to which there does not correspond a hundredfold of consolation and delight in this life, and it can truly say: "And pays every debt."

Stanza 3

O lamps of fire!
In whose splendors
The deep caverns of feeling,
Once obscure and blind,
Now give forth, so rarely, so exquisitely,
Both warmth and light to their beloved.

Commentary

The soul exalts and thanks its bridegroom in this stanza for the admirable favors it receives from its union with him. It states that by means of this union it receives abundant and lofty knowledge of God, which is all-loving, and which communicates light and love to its faculties and feeling. That which was once obscure and blind can now receive illumination and the warmth of love, as it does, so as to be able to give forth light and love to the one who illumined and filled it with love. True lovers are only content when they employ all that they are in themselves, are worth, have, and receive, in the beloved; and the greater all this is, the more satisfaction they receive in giving it. The soul rejoices on this account, because from the splendors and love it receives, it can shine brightly in the presence of its bridegroom and give him love. The verse follows:

O lamps of fire! First of all, it should be known that lamps possess two properties: they transmit both light and heat. To understand the nature of these lamps and how they shine and burn within the soul, it ought to be known that God in his unique and simple being is all the powers and grandeurs of his attributes. He is almighty, wise, and good; and he is merciful, just, powerful, and loving, and so on. And he is the other infinite attributes and powers of which we have no knowledge. Since he is all of this in his simple being, the soul views distinctly in him, when he is united with it and deigns to disclose this knowledge, all these powers and grandeurs, that is: omnipotence, wisdom, goodness, mercy, and so on. Since each of these attributes is the very being of God in his one and only *suppositum*, which is the Father, the Son, and the Holy Spirit, and since each one is God himself, who is infinite light or divine fire, we deduce that the soul, like God, gives forth light and warmth through each of these innumerable attributes. Each of these attributes is a lamp that enlightens it and transmits the warmth of love.

Insofar as the soul receives the knowledge of these attributes in only one act of this union, God himself is for it many lamps together, which illumine and impart warmth to it individually, for it has clear knowledge of each, and through this knowledge is inflamed in love. By means of all the lamps, the soul loves each individually, inflamed by each one and by all together, because all these attributes are one being, as we said. All these lamps are one lamp which, according to its powers and attributes, shines and burns like many lamps. Hence the soul in one act of knowledge of these lamps loves through each one and, in so doing, loves through them all together, bearing in that act the quality of love for each one and from each one, and from all together and for all together.

The splendor of this lamp of God's being, insofar as he is omnipotent, imparts light to the soul and the warmth of love of him according to his omnipotence. God is then to the soul a lamp of omnipotence which shines and bestows all knowledge in respect to this attribute. And the splendor of this lamp of God's being insofar as he is wisdom grants the soul light and the warmth of the love of god according to his wisdom. God is then a lamp of wisdom to it. And the splendor of this lamp insofar as it is goodness imparts to the soul light and the warmth of love according to his goodness. God is then a lamp of goodness to it. He is also to the soul a lamp of justice, fortitude, and mercy, and of all the other attributes that are represented to it together in God. The light communicated to it from all these attributes together is enveloped in the warmth of love of God by which it loves him because he is all these things. In this communication and manifestation of himself to the soul, which in my opinion is the greatest possible in this life, he is to it innumerable lamps giving forth knowledge and love of himself.

Moses beheld these lamps on Mount Sinai where, when God passed by, he prostrated himself on the ground and began to call out and enumerate some of them: "Emperor, Lord, God merciful, clement, patient, of much compassion, true, who keeps mercy unto thousands, who takes away iniquities and sins, no one is of himself innocent before you" [Exod. 34:6–7]. In this passage it is clear that the greatest attributes and powers Moses knew there in God were those of God's omnipotence, dominion, deity, mercy, justice, truth, and righteousness, which was the highest knowledge of God. Because love was communicated to him in accord with the knowledge, the delight of love and fruition he enjoyed were most sublime.

It is noteworthy that the delight the soul receives in the rapture of love, communicated by the fire of the light of these lamps, is wonderful and immense, for it is as abundant as it would be if it came from many lamps. Each lamp burns in love, and the warmth from each furthers the warmth of the other, and the flame of one, the flame of the other, just as the light of one sheds light on the other, because through each attribute the other is known. Thus all of them are one light and one fire, and each of them is one light and one fire.

Immensely absorbed in delicate flames, subtly wounded with love through each of them, and more wounded by all of them together, more alive in the love of the life of God, the soul perceives clearly that that love is proper to eternal life. Eternal life is the aggregation of all goods, and the soul somehow experiences this here and fully understands the truth of the bridegroom's assertion in the Song of

Songs, that the lamps of love are lamps of fire and of flames [Song of Sol. 8:6]. . . .

This feeling, then, of the soul that was once obscure, without this divine light, and blind through the soul's appetites and affections, has now together with the deep caverns of the soul's faculties become not only bright and clear, but like a resplendent light.

> Now give forth, so rarely, so exquisitely,
> Both warmth and light to their beloved.

When these caverns of the faculties are so wonderfully and marvelously pervaded with the admirable splendors of those lamps that are burning within them, they give forth to God in God with loving glory, besides their surrender to him, these very splendors they have received. Inclined in God toward God, having become enkindled lamps within the splendors of the divine lamps, they render the beloved the same light and heat they receive. In the very manner they receive it, they return it to the one who gave it, and with the same beauty in which it was given; just as the window when the sun shines on it, for it then too reflects the splendors. Yet the soul reflects the divine light in a more excellent way because of the active intervention of its will.

"So rarely, so exquisitely," means: in a way rare or foreign to every common thought, every exaggeration, and every mode and manner.

Corresponding to the exquisiteness or to the excellence with which the intellect receives the divine wisdom, being made one with God's intellect, is the excellence with which the soul gives this wisdom, for it cannot give it save according to the mode in which it was given.

And corresponding to the excellence by which the will is united to goodness is the excellence by which it gives in God the same goodness to God, for it only receives it in order to give it.

And, no more or less, according to the excellence by which it knows in the grandeur of God, being united to it, the soul shines and diffuses the warmth of love.

And according to the excellence of the divine attributes (fortitude, beauty, justice, and so on), which the beloved communicates, is the excellence with which the soul's feeling gives joyfully to him the very light and heat it receives from him. Having been made one with God, the soul is somehow God through participation. Although it is not God as perfectly as it will be in the next life, it is like the shadow of God. Being the shadow of God through this substantial transformation, it performs in this measure in God and through God what he through himself does in it. For the will of the two is one will, and thus God's operation and the soul's is one. Since God gives himself with a free and gracious will, so too the soul (possessing a will the more generous and free, the more it is united with God) gives to God, God himself in God; and this is a true and complete gift of the soul to God.

It is conscious there that God is indeed its own and that it possesses him by inheritance, with the right of ownership, as his adopted child, through the grace of his gift of himself. Having him for its own, it can give him and communicate him to whomever it wishes. Thus it gives him to its beloved, who is the very god who gave himself to it. By this donation it repays God for all it owes him, since it willingly gives as much as it receives from him.

Because the soul in this gift to God offers him the Holy Spirit, with voluntary surrender, as something of its own (so that God loves himself in the Holy Spirit as he deserves), it enjoys inestimable delight and fruition, seeing that it gives God something of its own which is suited to him according to his infinite being. Although it is true that the soul cannot give God again to himself, since in himself he is ever himself, nevertheless it does this truly and perfectly, giving all that was given it by him in order to repay love, which is to give as much as is given. And God, who could not be considered repaid with anything less, is considered repaid with that gift of the soul, and he accepts it gratefully as something it gives him of its own. In this very gift he loves it anew, and in the resurrender of God to the soul, the soul also loves as though again.

A reciprocal love is thus actually formed between God and the soul, like the marriage union and surrender, in which the goods of both (the divine essence which each possesses freely by reason of the voluntary surrender between them) are possessed by both together. They say to each other what the Son of God spoke to the Father through St. John: *Omnia mea tua sunt et tua mea sunt et clarificatus sum in eis* ("All my goods are yours and yours are mine, and I am glorified in them") [John 17:10]. In the next life this will continue unintermittently in perfect fruition, but in this state of union it occurs, although not as perfectly as in the next, when God produces in the soul this act of the transformation.

Clearly the soul can give this gift, even though the gift has greater entity than the soul's own being and capacity, for an owner of many nations and kingdoms, which have more entity than the owner does, can give them at will to anyone.

This is the soul's deep satisfaction and happiness: to see that it gives to God more than in itself it is worth; and this it does with that very divine light and divine heat and solitude. It does this in heaven by means of the light of glory and in this life by means of a highly illumined faith. Accordingly, the deep caverns of feeling give forth with rare excellence to their beloved heat and light together.

Stanza 4

> How gently and lovingly
> You wake in my heart,
> Where in secret you dwell alone;
> And in your sweet breathing,
> Filled with good and glory,
> How tenderly you swell my heart with love!

Commentary

And thus it is as though the soul were to say: "How gentle and loving (that is, extremely loving and gentle) is your awakening, O Word, Spouse, in the center and depth of my soul, which is its pure and intimate substance, in which secretly and silently, as its only lord, you dwell alone, not only as in your house, nor only as in your bed, but also as in my own heart, intimately and closely united to it. And how delicately you captivate me and arouse my affections toward you in the sweet breathing you produce in this awakening, a breathing delightful to me and full of good and glory."

The soul uses this comparison because its experience here is similar to that of one who upon awakening breathes deeply.

The verse follows:

> How gently and lovingly
> You wake in my heart.

There are many kinds of awakening that God effects in the soul, so many that we would never finish explaining them all. Yet this awakening of the Son of God, which the soul wishes to refer to here, is one of the most elevated and most beneficial. For this awakening is a movement of the Word in the substance of the soul containing such grandeur, dominion, glory, and intimate sweetness that it seems to the soul that all the balsams and fragrant spices and flowers of the world are commingled, stirred, and shaken so as to yield their sweet odor, and that all the kingdoms and dominions of the world and all the powers and virtues of heaven are moved; and not only this, but it also seems that all the virtues and substances and perfections and graces of every created thing glow and make the same movement all at once.

Since, as St. John says, "All things in him are life" [John 1:3–4], and, as the Apostle declares, "In him they live and are and move" [Acts 17:28], it follows that when, within the soul, this great Emperor moves (whose principality, as Isaiah says, he bears on his shoulders [Isa. 9:6]—which consists of the three spheres, celestial, terrestrial, and infernal, and the things contained in them—upholding them all, as St. Paul says [Heb. 1:3], with the word of his power), all things seem to move in unison. This happens in the same manner as when, at the movement of the earth, all material things in it move as though they were nothing. So it is when this Prince moves, who himself carries his court, instead of his court carrying him.

Even this comparison is most inadequate, for in this awakening they not only seem to move, but they all likewise disclose the beauties of their being, power, loveliness, and graces, and the root of their duration and life. For the soul is conscious of how all creatures, earthly and heavenly, have their life, duration, and strength in him, and it clearly realizes what he says in the book of Proverbs: "By me kings reign and princes rule and the mighty exercise justice and understand it" [Prov. 8:15–16]. Although it is indeed aware that these things are distinct from God, insofar as they have created being, nonetheless that which it understands of God, by his being all these things with infinite eminence, is such that it knows these things better in God's being than in themselves.

And here lies the remarkable delight of this awakening: the soul knows creatures through God and not God through creatures. This amounts to knowing the effects through their cause and not the cause through its effects. The latter is knowledge a posteriori, and the former is essential knowledge. . . .

Where in secret you dwell alone. The soul says he dwells in its heart in secret, because this sweet embrace is wrought in the depths of its substance.

It should be known that God dwells secretly in all souls and is hidden in their substance, for otherwise they would not last. Yet there is a difference, a great difference, in his dwelling in them. In some souls he dwells alone, and in others he does not dwell alone. Abiding in some, he is pleased; and in others, he is displeased. He lives in some as though in his own house, commanding and ruling everything; and in others as though a stranger in a strange house, where they do not permit him to give orders or do anything.

It is in that soul in which less of its own appetites and pleasures dwell that he dwells more alone, more pleased, and more as though in his own house, ruling and governing it. And he dwells more in secret, the more he dwells alone. Thus in this soul, in which neither any appetite nor other images or forms nor any affections for created things dwell, the beloved dwells secretly with an embrace so much the closer, more intimate, and interior, the purer and more alone the soul is to everything other than God. His dwelling is in secret, then, because the devil cannot reach the area of this embrace, nor can one's intellect understand how it occurs.

Yet it is not secret to the soul itself that has attained this perfection, for within itself it has the experience of this intimate embrace. It does not, however, always experience these awakenings, for when the beloved produces them, it seems to the soul that he is awakening in its heart, where before he remained as though asleep. Although it was experiencing and enjoying him, this took place as though with a loved one who is asleep, for knowledge and love are not communicated mutually while one is still asleep.

Oh, how happy is this soul that ever experiences God resting and reposing within it! Oh, how fitting it is for it to withdraw from things, flee from business matters, and live in immense tranquillity, so that it may not even with the slightest mote or noise disturb or trouble its heart, where the beloved dwells.

He is usually there, in this embrace with his bride, as though asleep in the substance of the soul. And it is very well aware of him and ordinarily enjoys him. Were he always awake within it, communicating knowledge and love, it would already be in glory. For if, when he does waken, scarcely opening his eyes, he has such an effect on the soul, what would it be like were he ordinarily in it fully awake?

Although he is not displeased with other souls that have not reached this union, for after all they are in the state of grace, yet insofar as they are not well disposed, his dwelling is secret to them, even though he does dwell in them. They do not experience him ordinarily, except when he grants them some delightful awakening. But such an awakening is not of this kind and high quality, nor is it comparable to these, nor as secret to the intellect and the devil, which are still able to understand something through the movements of the senses. For the senses are not fully annihilated until the soul reaches this union, and they still have some activity and movements concerning the spiritual, since they are not yet totally spiritual.

But in this awakening of the bridegroom in the perfect soul, everything that occurs and is caused is perfect, for he is the cause of it all. And in that awakening, which is as though one were to awaken and breathe, the soul feels a strange delight in the breathing of the

Holy Spirit in God, in which it is sovereignly glorified and taken with love. Hence it says in the subsequent verses:

> And in your sweet breathing,
> Filled with good and glory,
> How tenderly you swell my heart with love!

I do not desire to speak of this spiration, filled for the soul with good and glory and delicate love of God, for I am aware of being incapable of so doing; and were I to try, it might seem less than it is. It is a spiration that God produces in the soul, in which, by that awakening of lofty knowledge of the Godhead, he breathes the Holy Spirit in it in the same proportion as was its knowledge and understanding of him, absorbing it most profoundly in the Holy Spirit, rousing its love with divine excellence and delicacy according to what it beheld in him. Since the breathing is filled with good and glory, the Holy Spirit, through this breathing, filled the soul with good and glory, in which he enkindled it in love of himself, indescribably and incomprehensibly, in the depths of God, to whom be honor and glory forever and ever. Amen.

ABOUT THE EDITOR

HarperCollins Spiritual Classics Series Editor Emilie Griffin has long been interested in the classics of the devotional life. She has written a number of books on spiritual formation and transformation, including *Clinging: The Experience of Prayer* and *Wilderness Time: A Guide to Spiritual Retreat*. With Richard J. Foster she coedited *Spiritual Classics: Selected Readings on the Twelve Spiritual Disciplines*. Her latest book is *Wonderful and Dark Is this Road: Discovering the Mystic Path*. She is a board member of Renovaré and leads retreats and workshops throughout the United States. She and her husband William live in Alexandria, Louisiana.

THE CLASSICS OF **WESTERN SPIRITUALITY**
A LIBRARY OF THE GREAT SPIRITUAL MASTERS

These volumes contain original writings of universally acknowledged teachers within the Catholic, Protestant, Eastern Orthodox, Jewish, Islamic, and American Indian traditions.

The Classics of Western Spirituality unquestionably provide the most in-depth, comprehensive, and accessible panorama of Western mysticism ever attempted. From the outset, the Classics has insisted on the highest standards for these volumes, including new translations from the original languages, and helpful introductions and other aids by internationally recognized scholars and religious thinkers, designed to help the modern reader to come to a better appreciation of these works that have nourished the three monotheistic faiths for centuries.

The Cloud of Unknowing	*Teresa of Avila*	*John of the Cross*	*John and Charles Wesley*
Edited and Introduced by James Walsh	Edited and Introduced by Kieran Kavanaugh, O.C.D.	Edited and Introduced by Kieran Kavanaugh, O.C.D.	Edited and Introduced by Frank Whaling
0-8091-2332-0 $22.95	0-8091-2254-5 $22.95	0-8091-2839-X $21.95	0-8091-2368-1 $26.95

For more information on the
CLASSICS OF WESTERN SPIRITUALITY, contact Paulist Press
(800) 218-1903 • www.paulistpress.com